CANADIAN CON ARTISTS

CANADIAN CON ARTISTS

Lisa Wojna

QUAGMIRE
PRESS

The Publisher: Quagmire Press Ltd.
Website: www.quagmirepress.com

Library and Archives Canada Cataloguing in Publication

Wojna, Lisa, 1962–
    Canadian con artists / Lisa Wojna.

Includes bibliographical references.
ISBN 978-1-926695-06-8

    1. Swindlers and swindling—Canada—Biography. 2. Fraud—Canada.
I. Title.

HV6699.C3W63 2009   364.16'3092271   C2009-905934-7

Project Director: Hank Boer
Project Editor: Pat Price
Cover Image: iStockphoto/Joseph Jean Rolland Dubé

We gratefully acknowledge the support of the Alberta Foundation for the Arts for our publishing program.

PC: P1

Contents

Dedication

For Jada: Always go with your gut.

Acknowledgements

Creating a book involves far more than writing something your editor or publisher would like to see in print. Every topic worth researching and writing requires a willingness on the writer's part to wade through mountains of material, much of which has been previously published in print, radio and broadcast. With that in mind, I owe a debt of gratitude to the journalists, authors, bloggers and editors who first brought some of these stories to light, either online or in their respective publications, and to the producers and directors of documentaries and news segments; they provided a visual connection that helped me form a deeper understanding of the con artists I was writing about, as well as their victims.

I'd like to say thank you to the staff of the Wetaskiwin Public Library, who are always willing to help me find some obscure bit of information on the latest topic I'm researching. Without their efforts, those hidden gems would have remained hidden and some of these stories the lesser for it.

Thank you to my family, who do more than just put up with me—they believe in me. Thank you to my mentor, Faye. And a special thanks to my editor, Pat Price. She was able to take my original manuscript, with all its good intentions and often unwieldy tales, and pull everything together into the tight document you have before you. She not only ironed out the many of the kinks of my first attempts at telling these important stories but has also helped breathe life into them.

And finally, to the staff of Quagmire Press, who have allowed me to pen three volumes for them on topics near and dear to my heart, thank you for your commitment to publishing stories about crime that are designed not to glorify criminal actions but to make a difference in people's lives.

Introduction

~

It's immoral to let a sucker keep his money.

−attributed to William "Canada Bill" Jones,
three-card monte con artist

There's a new lady in your social circle; we'll call her Sally. She's full of energy, a go-getter with great ideas on just about everything and a pure joy to have at any party. Sally became everyone's best friend the moment she moved into the neighbourhood. You've heard there's money somewhere in her background, but, from what you can see, she lives the epitome of a modest lifestyle. She has a great career and a husband who dotes on her, and everyone agrees she's a great listener: she hangs onto your every word and is always asking if she can lend a hand. She is generous to a fault, and if you've ever lunched with her, you'll know she usually plays a tug of war over the bill. She usually wins.

One day, Sally comes to you, visibly upset about something. She says she is the oldest of three girls, the daughter of a relationship that ended years before her mother married her stepfather. She confesses that her sisters have never liked her and that, since her stepfather's death, they have ostracized her from the family. Now, her widowed mother is confused because of Alzheimer's disease and is dying of cancer. Sally wants to visit her mother, but her sisters won't let her.

You ask Sally if she thinks her sisters will influence her mother's will. But Sally shuts you down. Money isn't everything, she says; she just misses her mother and wishes she and her sisters were friends.

You are outraged. You feel like you've known this woman all your life, and you just can't understand how her sisters could treat her so badly. Now comes the clincher. Sally tells you that she's got herself a good lawyer in the distant city where her mother lives. This lawyer will help her in this difficult family situation. The problem is that he's asked for a $3000 retainer, and he needs payment by the week's end or he'll decline her case—money up front is quite common in a family-law situation and, besides, he's a very busy man. The lawyer knows Sally's situation inside out, and Sally desperately needs to pay the lawyer so she can see her mother before she dies. But she doesn't have the money, and, because she's new in town, the banks won't give her a loan. Sally is desperate. "What if...what if my mother dies before I can make it to her bedside?" she asks.

You're touched by Sally's situation, and you know you can loan her the money she needs. With the economy the way it is, your money isn't earning much interest sitting in the bank. And you have absolutely no doubt Sally will pay you back. You also know if the situation were reversed, Sally would do the same thing for you, so you offer to loan her the money for the lawyer and enough cash to pay for a return plane ticket.

Shortly after Sally boards her flight, you find out that she's hit up two or three of your other friends for a similar loan. Between you all, Sally's retainer and return ticket have apparently cost about $20,000. You're confused. As the days turn into weeks and months, and no one hears from Sally, you know you've been duped. You also realize there's so much you don't know about Sally. Where did she say her mother lived? What was Sally's last name? Where did she work? And you never did meet her husband—he always seemed to be away on business.

Perhaps you're scoffing at this example. You say you'd never be taken for such a fool.

Think again.

Phineas Taylor Barnum, more commonly known by his initials P.T. and one of the greatest showmen of all time, coined the phrase "there is a sucker born every minute." One just has to review the RCMP's Scams and Fraud website to recognize that this must be true. Although Barnum's description is a little harsh, Canadians—and people in general—succumb to some kind of fraud more often than you might think. Fortunately, we're becoming increasingly aware of scams and about the importance of knowing how to protect ourselves from becoming victims. For example, according to the RCMP's *Personal Information and Scams Protection—A Canadian Practical Guide*, a 2006 Ipsos-Reid survey suggests that at least "73 percent of Canadians are worried about becoming victims of identity fraud," and "only 33 percent of Canadians feel that they are well educated on personal information and scam protection." If this is the case, why do we continue to fall victim to fraud?

In 1943, Abraham Maslow wrote about his take on what makes most of us tick in his paper *A Theory of Human Motivation*. Commonly known as Maslow's "hierarchy of needs," the study looked at healthy, educated, well-rounded individuals and revealed that all humans have five basic "needs": physiological, safety, love and belonging, esteem and self-actualization. Maslow defined the first four of those requirements as "deficiency needs." Not meeting those needs can cause some degree of suffering, but along our path to self-actualization, we can easily get stuck in one of those deficiency needs.

For example, striving to provide for your financial security is healthy. So, when someone suggests you invest with the Wall Street firm of Bernard L. Madoff Investment Securities LLC, and you know of Madoff's reputation and his apparent philanthropy, you can't imagine a better opportunity. Of course, we now know that even someone as prominent as Bernie Madoff isn't always what he appears to be. After pleading guilty in March 2009 to 11 felonies and being named as the perpetrator behind a Ponzi scheme that has been described as possibly the "largest investment fraud in Wall Street history," Madoff is, as of this writing, making his permanent home at the Federal Correctional Complex in Butner, North Carolina.

It's also easy to get caught up in building your personal nest egg to extreme proportions, just in case the market collapses or you lose your job. The desire to make a quick buck, especially when the economy is anemic and job prospects are limited, is another weakness scammers exploit when presenting those tantalizing propositions. A few years ago, a friend tried to talk me into joining an investment opportunity that promised huge returns. All I needed to do was hand over the money and wait for the payout that would come in the not-too-distant future. She expected to receive a cheque for several thousand dollars more than her initial investment of $5000. It was legitimate, she assured me. Even police and RCMP officers had apparently invested in the "club," so it must be legitimate—or so she'd been told.

As it turned out, my friend was one of the estimated 4000 Canadian and U.S. residents who'd invested as much as $400 million in a Ponzi scheme that resulted in at least two Alberta men, 55-year-old Milowe Brost and 66-year-old Gary Sorenson, facing charges of fraud. The police made the arrests after more than three years of investigative efforts. Sadly, many investors never saw any money, and, in one case, the sister of one unfortunate investor, who'd allegedly shelled out more than $300,000, blamed the scheme for causing her sister's death.

Fear is another prime motivator when it comes to separating people from their hard-earned cash. It's one of the reasons why "phishing"—sending out bogus emails that appear to be from a legitimate financial institution asking for personal information—is so profitable for scammers. That information can be used for any number of cons, from identity theft to what has been called "white card fraud"—a scam that uses the information to clone ATM cards and clean out a victim's bank accounts.

Scammers touch almost every corner of society; no one is exempt from being targeted. And many of these scammers aren't just clever and conniving, they're dangerous. A cursory glance at media headlines across the country culled randomly over just a few months in 2009 is enough to make even the most trusting person cautious:

- "Do not get burned by furnace fraud"

  —Tribune, Williams Lake, BC

- "Con artist scams Tillsonburg store"

  —Sentinel-Review, Woodstock, Ontario

- "Email scam plays on musicians' dreams"

  —CBC News

- "Israeli art scam hits Calgary"

  —CBC News

- "3 years for fraudster with 'trail of victims'"

  —Ottawa Sun

- "Man charged in Internet dating scheme fraud"

  —*Ottawa Citizen*

- "Ponzi scheme led to victim's suicide...INVESTMENT SCAM: Kelowna woman lost money, hope"

  —*Calgary Sun*

As the stories that follow reveal, most con artists initially come across as anxious to please. They make a great show of going out of their way to help everyone they know. They are full of promises that, in the end, fall short of expectations, and they plug into our basic human emotions. Many of their cons are built around plausible, if not necessarily probable, stories.

It's often been said that life is stranger than fiction, so when someone introduces himself as a Rockefeller and offers to be your friend, you'd like to believe him. Knowing a Rockefeller is a great boost to a person's self-esteem, and who knows what financial connections the relationship might inspire? We might laugh about the idea while watching a movie like *Wedding Crashers*, but con artists around the world have conducted similar scams and walked away, leaving financial ruin and destruction in their path.

Unlike the preceding tale of Sally, the comedy *Wedding Crashers* or the exploits of entertainers like P.T. Barnum, this book is not a work of fiction. Every story represents an assortment of real people who were victimized financially, emotionally, mentally and sometimes even physically so that the individual or individuals perpetrating the scam received some kind of compensation, be it money or success or power and control.

However, this book is not intended to create paranoia. Not everyone out there is like Sally. We still need to be able to extend a certain amount of trust to the people who come into our lives daily and to reach out to help where we can. Without some level of trust, we, as a civilized society, would cease to exist. As American actor and director Frank Hall Crane once said, "You may be deceived if you trust too much, but you will live in torment if you don't trust enough."

Chapter One

The Art of the Con

I t's strange that something so potentially devastating
goes by the name "confidence game" and is performed by
a "confidence artist," as if the entire experience is just for
fun and the individuals directing the game are uniquely gifted,
such as renowned Canadian painters Tom Thomson or Emily
Carr. But the terms describe the subject of this book perfectly.

William Thompson is given the distinction of being the
first person in recorded history to be labelled a "confidence
man." On July 8, 1849, the *New York Herald* published a story
in the "Police Intelligence" section under the headline "Arrest of
the Confidence Man." The story explained how Thompson, who
appeared to be an elegant gentleman, approached other well-
dressed strangers on the street and, after a friendly chat, asked
them, "Have you confidence in me to trust me with your watch
until tomorrow?" Because of the familiar way he spoke to his
victims, they believed they must have known Thompson in the
past. Embarrassed by apparently forgetting an old acquaintance,
these victims usually went along with Thompson, handing over
their expensive gold watches. Although, by today's standards,
this might be considered nothing more than a petty offence,

Thompson apparently made his living this way—and judging by the newspaper's description of his appearance, it seems he made a fairly good living indeed.

Although there are variations to the con "games" a fraudster can pull off, these confidence artists all have one thing in common—they lay the groundwork for their scams by first gaining the confidence of their potential victims. The level of confidence required varies with the scam, but some degree of trust between the scammer and victim is essential for the scam to work. It takes a talented individual to garner the kind of unwavering confidence necessary to succeed at this game—it takes the skills of a true artist.

A con artist doesn't target everyone he or she meets, however. They're professionals at reading the masses, learning the individual weaknesses of the people they encounter and assessing if their personality will meld well with a potential victim's. Con artists observe their environment and the movements of those who come into their lives and insert themselves where they think they'd be most welcome and, therefore, most successful. Once they've chosen their victims, con artists typically show no cracks in their armour. They think very highly of themselves and, really, they have to, if they want to gain the confidence of their victims.

As they perpetrate their schemes, con artists live every moment of their story. Like pathological liars, they are so invested in the moment, they believe the fantasy they're living.

For that period of time, they *are* your best friend, that high-powered financier with the surefire investment opportunity or the woman whose family has turned their backs on her. Once these schemers have cast their nets and pulled in their catch, they disappear as quickly as they appeared and begin re-creating themselves somewhere else. And throughout the entire experience, they will feel no guilt whatsoever.

In many ways, the manipulative, self-absorbed con artist appears to be unable to conform to societal standards and rarely plans for his life and work and relationships. He or she is in constant need of stimulation, is impulsive and quick to move from one relationship to another and exhibits many signs of what psychologists call a sociopath. A confidence artist is in perfect control of his situation. He knows that what he is doing is wrong but does it anyway. He recognizes the potential devastation he will cause in people's lives and might even blame his victims for falling for his wiles in the first place.

Life in the confidence game is more varied than a few words could possibly explain, and the stories in this book are just a few examples of scams that were perpetrated by Canadians or by foreigners who spent time in our country. Following is an abbreviated outline of the kinds of scams and frauds you might come across. I venture to say that everyone who reads this book is familiar with at least one person whose life was affected by one of these confidence games.

STREET CONS

Many of us have been approached by a street person asking for spare change. Sometimes, the individual looks needy, and you can't help but dig deep into your pockets and grab whatever loose coins you can find. Ask a dozen different people how they feel about panhandling and you'll get a dozen different answers. Personally, I like to give if I can. It is quite possible that in doing so I'll have been conned and the individual I've just handed my hard-earned cash to is a lot better off than I'll ever be—we've all heard no end of urban legends about just such a thing happening. However, I'm aware of the potential risk, and if I have the money to give at the time, I do so. Still, it could be argued that someone playing on the empathy of people walking to and from work isn't fair. It's a deception in its own right.

A twist on the panhandler is the self-professed deaf person attempting to sell alphabet cards. It's only human to want to give a few dollars to the unfortunate individual with whom who you can't even communicate. But be wary. Although some deaf persons do make their living this way, it is not a fundraising method condoned by the Canadian Association for the Deaf. It is also quite easy for a hearing person to acquire these cards and play the role of a deaf person for the sole purpose of making money.

"Street cons," so named because these cons are performed on street sidewalks, are also referred to as "short cons" because they're performed quickly before the perpetrator disappears. These kinds of cons are typically about making a quick buck.

Like the panhandler begging for money for his next meal, the interaction between the victim and con artist is so fleeting that, when asked, it's often difficult for a victim to provide law enforcement with a description. That's why some of the more elaborate street swindles can make a con artist a pretty good living; he walks away without divulging anything about his identity.

THREE-CARD MONTE

It's a sunny day. You're walking along a busy street full of vendors and buskers when you notice a couple of people huddled around a makeshift table and a dealer shifting and throwing cards. "Whoa!" calls one of the men, as the dealer flips a card. The dealer hands the lucky man a few bills, and the other gives him a pat on the back. Curiosity pulls you in, but don't let it get you placing any bets. You will lose.

What you've observed is called three-card monte. This "game" is a short con, because the dealer can set up and move on in a matter of minutes. Typically, a dealer pulls off the three-card monte with the assistance of one or two compatriots known as shills. The dealer stands behind a table or a simple cardboard box and shows those gathered the three cards he has in his hands. Two are identical—two jacks, for example. The third card is usually an ace or queen of hearts. The object of the game is to identify the third or winning card after the dealer places the cards upside down and shuffles them around the table.

One shill will make a show of winning over and over again, laughing at the easy money he's pulling in, while the second shill pulls up alongside the "mark" or "sucker"—that's you—and says he just can't believe the other guy's luck. You decide to give it a try, and you lose. You try a few more times, and you lose each time. Before you get too frustrated, the dealer makes a big show of having seen the police and packs up his cards and leaves. The shills also disappear, and you're left standing alone and a bit dazed, wondering what you'd just participated in.

One of the earliest three-card monte con men to make an appearance and hone his skills in Canada was William Jones. Born in Yorkshire, England, sometime in the 1800s, Jones travelled to Canada with friend and fellow con man Dick Cady. Jones was in this country long enough to earn the name "Canada Bill" before moving on to more exciting possibilities south of the border. In time, he hooked up with George Devol, considered one of the "greatest riverboat (gamblers) in the history of the Mississippi River." When he retired, Devol wrote the book, *Forty Years a Gambler on the Mississippi*, a long and winding tale about his gambling exploits; in it, he describes his relationship with his friend and colleague Canada Bill:

> ...*a character one might travel the length and breadth of the land and never find his match, or run across his equal.... For hours he would sit in his chair, twisting his hair in little ringlets. Then I used to say, "Bill is studying up some new devilment." ...Canada was*

a slick one… Canada was, under all his hypocritical appearance, a regular card shark, and could turn monte with the best of them. He was my partner for a number of years, and many are the suckers we roped in, and many the huge rolls of bills we corralled.

Although you don't often see three-card monte on Canadian streets, dealers pop up every now and again in some of our bigger cities. And if you find yourself in a major U.S. city—New York, for example—you will likely notice a few of these gigs set up on one street or another. Never give it a try. You will always lose. A good dealer can even confuse his shills, and not even the best of luck can save you! To add insult to injury, according to one New York City website, a secondary objective of the three-card monte dealer and his shills is to pick the pockets of those who gather around to watch. It's best to keep your eyes focused elsewhere and just walk on by.

BAIT AND SWITCH

This simple but effective scheme involves what appears to be a straightforward retail sale: a product is advertised for an extremely low price—so low, in fact, that the item won't make the seller any money. Because many reputable stores offer "loss leaders" from time to time, in an effort to pull customers in, a sale offering huge discounts doesn't raise alarm bells. But in the bait and switch con, once the buyer is hooked, the seller feigns surprise at suddenly learning that the advertised product is out of stock. The consumer is understandably disappointed, until the seller offers a replacement item. Although the replacement product, which is often almost identical to the original item, is being offered at a considerably higher cost, the buyer orders it anyway.

It's perfectly legitimate at times for a seller to run out of a sale item, but when the seller advertises a blockbuster sale with no intention of providing the merchandise for that price, the interaction becomes a bait and switch scheme.

Laws surrounding fair advertising are complex, and even reputable companies have had some of their promotions challenged. On September 28, 2009, the *Austin Business Journal* reported that Dell Inc. had settled a lawsuit filed by the New York Attorney General's office. The Dell defendants in the case, Round Rock–based Dell (NASDAQ: DELL) and Dell Financial Services, "agreed to pay $4 million in restitution, penalties and costs to settle charges of fraudulent and deceptive business practices when doing business with New York consumers." The settlement came about after customers complained that Dell was advertising "no interest" financing but didn't always follow through, even when customers were told they qualified for the promotion. The company was also accused of reneging on its promise of rebates and failure to follow through on its warranty service.

Bait and switch tactics can be used in other ways as well, such as when an employer advertising a job opening elaborates on the working conditions, compensation and benefits of the job then fails to make good on the promises once an individual has been hired. Whenever entering any kind of business transaction, whether in retail sales or applying for a job, make sure you're getting exactly what you expect. Always read the fine print.

In Canada, the Competition Bureau oversees laws governing business conduct in this country. It is against the Competition Act for retailers in Canada to advertise a sale product without having "reasonable quantities" available for consumers. This business scam affects both consumers and other retailers. Should you believe you've come across a bait and switch scam, contact the Competition Bureau in Gatineau, Québec.

PIGEON DROP

Ed Grabianowski, a freelance writer from Buffalo, New York, tells the story of what he calls "the pedigree dog scam." This elaborate scam requires two individuals and just about any kind of canine. Playing on the basic instinct of greed, one of the con artists walks into a pub or by a street vendor with his beloved four-legged friend in tow and asks the attending employee for permission to tie up the dog nearby and if he wouldn't mind keeping an eye on it while he rushes to an urgent appointment. The con man promises the bartender or street vendor that he will be gone for only a few minutes. The shaggy pup is a sweet, reserved fellow, and the victim sees no reason why it can't just sit there for a few minutes. After all, it adds a little variety to the day.

Shortly after the dog owner leaves, another inconspicuous-looking man happens by and starts admiring the dog; it's a rare breed, he says, then asks the vendor if he might buy it from him. The man is willing to pay thousands of dollars for the pup, and when the victim hears how much the man is willing to fork over, he gets a brilliant idea. He tells the interested fellow to come back in an hour—he has to talk it over with his wife, or whatever. When the original con man returns, the vendor offers him everything he has for the pooch. He tells con man number one that the "beautiful dog" is so calming and charming and he never knew how much he missed having a dog. Making every show of reluctance, con man number one takes the money from the victim, gives his pooch one last hug and waltzes away with a pretty nice payday, even if he has to share it with his partner.

The clincher, of course, is that the dog is a mutt and was likely picked up at the SPCA. It certainly isn't worth the money paid out by the victim. When the second con man doesn't return to buy the dog, the victim finally catches on to the fact that, aside from becoming the new owner of a sad little pup, he's had the wool pulled over his eyes.

The pedigree dog scam is a variation of a con game commonly known as the "pigeon drop." Here's how it works. You're working at the front desk of a hotel and someone calls saying she's forgotten a briefcase filled with important work documents in the hotel coffee shop. While you're on the phone, a patron walks out of the coffee shop and brings you a small briefcase he says he found under his table. You share the news with your caller, who is overjoyed by the news and offers to give the gent who found her case a substantial reward. The caller says she'll stop by later, but the Good Samaritan from the coffee shop can't wait around. He suggests leaving the briefcase with you, and the two of you can split the reward. You have no problem with that, so you open the till—or your purse—and hand over the equivalent of half of the reward money. The man from the coffee shop leaves with his cash. The woman on the phone never shows up. And you're in a lot of trouble with your boss.

According to Paul J. Zak, author of "How to Run a Con" in *Psychology Today,* the pigeon drop is successful because the con artist puts his confidence in the victim, giving him a sense of security; he's confident that he's in no danger of losing anything and that the person he's dealing with is honourable.

Both the pedigree dog and pigeon drop take only moments to pull off, leaving victims with little or no concrete information for police to take action. Even if the victims do provide substantial information, these con games are often perpetrated by someone just passing through or who doesn't usually frequent that part of the city. By the time the police are called in, these con artists are on their way to pull off another scam somewhere else.

GOOD SAMARITAN SCAM

It's not unusual to be approached on the street by tourists, perhaps, or a couple celebrating a special occasion, asking you to snap a photo for them. You oblige—after all, it takes only a few seconds, so you fiddle a little with the camera and the background for the photo, and, once you've taken the picture, they thank you and depart. Usually, the interaction passes without incident. But enterprising con artists have used this scenario to defraud that Good Samaritan, who is almost always a woman, of her money.

This scam requires three people to work it: the "couple" requesting the photo and a third person hovering nearby. The couple makes sure to pose in such a way that the woman's back is to her purse. While they are occupying the victim, the third person picks up the purse and hides it in his briefcase. Once the picture is taken, the pair thank the woman and, making every effort to appear as enamoured with each other as possible, they meander off.

That's when the woman notices that her purse is missing and panics. The third con artist, whose briefcase contains the purse, has remained nearby and now rushes to her side. Hearing that her purse has been stolen, the man offers to lend her his cell phone, so she can alert her bank of the theft. He even offers to dial the bank for her.

Too distressed to think properly and grateful for the offer, the woman takes the phone and asks the bank staff to freeze her accounts. First, however, she provides them with her personal information, which is always requested to ensure that the bank staff are actually speaking to a legitimate client. What the woman doesn't know is that the cell phone call has been routed to a nearby van. The couple she'd photographed just moments earlier are in the van, taking the call and noting her information. When the call is completed, the woman thinks she has done everything she can to protect herself when, in reality, she has opened the door for the con artists to empty her bank accounts and max out her credit cards.

There are many examples of what has been called the "Good Samaritan scam," and they all involve someone who professes to be in some kind of trouble or needs a quick favour and an individual willing to help.

One online watchdog described the tale of an elderly woman who, several years before safety precautions were available to banking customers, agreed to deposit money into her bank account as a favour to a stranger who'd apparently just been robbed. He explained to the woman that all the money he had left in the world—a total of $2500—was in his possession, and he wanted to put it in the bank for safekeeping. But the bank was closed for the weekend, and, because his bank card had also been stolen, he had no way of getting his money into the bank. The stranger promised the elderly woman $100 for helping him out. Because she had helped the man count the money before he stuffed it into an envelope and handed it to her for depositing into the ATM, she felt confident his plight was genuine. What she didn't realize was that he'd switched envelopes—she'd deposited nothing but paper. The stranger had also watched her enter her PIN, and, when she least expected it, he grabbed her card and ran. Of course, this happened over a long weekend, leaving the elderly woman with no way to get in touch with her bank and the man with four days to withdraw her money.

THE PYRAMID SCHEME

This is your lucky day.

I have a fail-proof way to make money, and guess what—I'm going to share my idea with you!

This will require a small investment on your part, but trust me; I will make your money work for you. In no time at all your investment will double, maybe even triple, in size.

I'm also quite convinced that, as you think this through, you'll want to share this great opportunity with your friends and family members. In fact, it will benefit you to do so. The more people you attract with this offer, the faster, and larger, your payout.

If you've ever been approached with this kind of offer and declined, count yourself among the lucky—you just walked away from getting caught in a pyramid scheme.

The pyramid scheme is a popular vehicle used by con artists to part people from their money. It's lucrative for the fraudster, not so lucrative for the investor.

Because of its popularity, creative minds around the world have developed variations on the theme in an effort to confuse potential investors and appear legitimate; as investors become increasingly savvy, con artists become increasingly creative.

One case in point made its debut in Canada a few years ago. On quick review, JewelWay International appeared legitimate. Like legitimate multilevel marketing companies (Avon, Tupperware and Mary Kay, for example), which rely on the method of home-based sales through independent consultants, JewelWay provided sales representatives with a sales kit and several samples of jewellery for an initial fee. These sellers were then encouraged to promote the product by getting other people to buy into the company as representatives. Although it sounds legitimate to this point, this is where the "pyramid" part of the company comes into play—the amount of money the reps made actually selling the jewellery was quite small; the real money was made by bringing on more and more sales representatives who, in turn, brought in others. It was a simple and straightforward business deal that made its originators a lot of money and left many others with a caseload of what amounted to expensive costume jewellery.

In 1997, the U.S. Federal Trade Commission slammed JewelWay International with a $5 million settlement, saying the company represented an "illegal multi-level marketing plan or pyramid scheme" and explained that in "a pyramid scheme there is almost no emphasis on making retail sales of products to persons who are not participants in the program"—in a nutshell, that described JewelWay.

THE PONZI SCHEME

Charles Ponzi was born in Italy in 1882 and arrived in Boston, Massachusetts, on a drizzly November day in 1903. He was a young man of just 21, with nothing more than a scant $2.50 in his pocket and an admonishment from his elders back home to "Go and make a fortune and then come back." The general perception seemed to be that fortunes could easily be made in North America, but for a lad who couldn't speak the language, acquiring a decent job that he'd enjoy and would pay well was impossible. And so, it wasn't long before young Ponzi was looking for inventive ways to make money and to climb the economic ladder considerably faster than the menial jobs he'd managed to land would allow.

He arrived in Montréal, Québec, in July 1907 and spent some time in Canadian cells for supposedly forging a cheque, among other things, before returning to the U.S. in 1919. Not long after his arrival in Boston, Ponzi hatched a master plan that not only made him a very rich man but also inevitably destroyed his life.

Ponzi discovered he could purchase International Postal Reply Coupons (IPRCs) from other countries at low prices and resell them for a profit. He canvassed people interested in investing their money in his new venture and promised, in exchange, a profit of as much as a 40 percent in just 90 days. As more and more people clamoured to get involved, Ponzi sweetened the pot by promising a 50 percent return in 45 days and a 100 percent return for those who willing to part with their money for 90 days.

Initially, he paid off the earlier investors with money collected from later investors—the "classic earmark of a Ponzi scheme," according to the North American Securities Administrators Association (NASAA)—but, before long, the payments ceased. Some estimates suggest that Ponzi hustled investors for an amazing $10 million and that a mere $30 was tracked to the actual purchase of IPRCs.

Ponzi's ride in the high life was short-lived. When suspicion fell on Ponzi and his business, investors got nervous and began to demand their money. Ponzi was eventually arrested and his scam exposed. After spending some time in a Massachusetts jail, he was deported to Italy.

Almost a century later, con artists still rely on the "robbing Peter to pay Paul" scam to make money, and people still fall for it. The NASAA warns the public that Ponzi schemes continue to be popular and that people continue to buy into them because they promise a lucrative, sure-bet investment.

They never are.

INVESTMENT FRAUD

Some savvy con artists build a rapport with their potential victims and, once they've gained their confidence, offer them a great business opportunity. Once a relationship is formed, the victim can't imagine that a friend would be anything less than truthful. And so, a deal, sometimes more than one, is made between the con artist and his victim. The con artist might provide a litany of excuses for why the return on his friend's investment hasn't come through yet—he's likely operating other scams, and disappearing just then wouldn't be convenient. But rest assured, when the victim is ready to push for his money back, this fraudster friend will have disappeared. Christophe Rocancourt said he made $40 million during his time as an active con artist, and much of that money was collected through just such a scam. (See "Playing Like a Rockefeller—A Man of Great Expectations," page 89.)

PHISHING FOR PROFIT

The Internet and email have proven to be stellar areas for con artists to gain access to personal and banking information. Often, contact is made with an individual under the guise of what appears to be a legitimate business. For example, an email might look like official bank correspondence or something from a popular website, such as Amazon.com or eBay, warning you of a scam. Usually, this email asks you to answer a question or two or to confirm something by clicking on a link, and its originator is relying on you to believe the request is credible. It never is. Banks and reputable businesses do not make client contact in this way. Banks usually only contact clients about important information through regular mail or their Internet banking sites. A reputable business will rarely, if ever, contact clients and, if it does, never through email.

HOW TO PROTECT YOURSELF

There's no way to guarantee that you'll never fall for a scam at some point in your life. But you can take precautions to limit your vulnerability. Here are a few tips for consumers:

- "If something sounds too good to be true, it usually is." There's a reason why that's an old and familiar adage—it's true. Even if you're desperate to take advantage of a great investment opportunity or get in on a "surefire thing," tell the person making the offer that you first need to do some research. If the response is "this is a now-or-never opportunity," walk away. A legitimate business transaction is never a high-pressure activity.

- Never give personal information to telephone or door-to-door solicitors. Nonprofit organizations raised funds this way in the past, but, now, most offer increasingly safer fundraising options for their supporters, such as electronic fundraising through an organization's website and using direct mail.

- Don't be fooled by "good news" mail. There was a time when businesses, such as Publisher's Clearing House, offered legitimate chances at winning fairly substantial prizes. Today, some mail-in sweepstakes offer large prizes for a price—patrons are supposed to send money or purchase something. This is often a scam.

- When using your credit card to purchase something, don't let it out of your sight. Ask the cashier to return it as soon as it has been swiped and the signature checked.

- Where the signature bar appears on the back of your credit card, make a note that cashiers are required to ask for identification. This is sometimes inconvenient when you're in a hurry, but, should you lose your credit card, it could save you a lot of money.

- Identity theft is a huge concern, and there is a lot of information about who we are on our computers. To protect yourself from identity theft, make sure your computer's hard drive is completely destroyed before recycling an old computer.

- Never carry your social insurance number with you. These numbers can provide a significant amount of personal information to the wrong people. Birth certificates should also be kept in a safe place and not carried in your wallet.

- Protect your debit card. Should a thief get his hands on your bank card and your personal identification number, he can easily make a false deposit with an empty deposit envelope or use the bank card to access accounts and make withdrawals.

- No doubt you remember the Nigerian money-transfer scam—those sporadic requests for information, usually a bank number, so some oppressed person from a third-world country could transfer money into our bank accounts. For the privilege of allowing this transaction, you'd receive considerable financial compensation. Greed is a huge motivator for becoming involved in these kinds of opportunities. But often survival, or at the very least, an opportunity to ease life's load, is all it takes to entice someone into taking a chance on something that's not quite above-board. This request for information, and any others like it, must be ignored. Incidentally, a resurgence of these emails is occurring at the time of this writing.

- Be wary of someone selling you something online. Scammers can even infiltrate legitimate businesses, so review all the information you receive thoroughly before making a purchase, ask lots of questions and be sure all your questions are answered.

- Never give your credit card number to a telephone solicitor.

- Be wary of door-to-door salesmen offering to inspect your furnace or provide home repairs, even salesmen with fancy vans decked out with company logos. Check out every transaction before signing on the dotted line.

- Ask plenty of questions, and demand documentation for everything. A business should provide contact information that includes a physical address, not a post office box. Ask for a business card, and walk your salesperson to the vehicle, so you can write down the licence plate number. If the situation is legitimate, the salesperson won't flinch. If it's not, you probably won't be hearing from him any time in the near future.

For more information on how to protect yourself, log onto the Industry Canada website and, in particular, the Office of Consumer Affairs. Research potential business investments with the Canadian Better Business Bureau. Contact the RCMP for information on any opportunity you aren't sure of, and download a copy of the publication *Personal Information and Scams Protection—A Canadian Practical Guide*. You might even consider calling local investment brokers or lawyers for their take on a situation. There is no such thing as being too cautious.

Chapter Two

The Power Behind the Persona
SALIM MOHAMMED DAMJI

~

I had to go along with it. I had no choice. They used my
family as bait.... They would force me to buy things, lux-
ury items, to make it look like I was doing the fraud.

–Salim Mohammed Damji in an interview with CTV News,
W-FIVE, November 2002

FLASHBACK TO ANOTHER ERA

In 1975, I was just 13 years old. I was already convicted in
my faith, committed in my beliefs—so much so that my
mother, who didn't attend church, and my father, who'd
had some pretty harrowing experiences in his home parish in
Poland, were convinced that I was destined to be exploited by
some religious charlatan.

On weekends, when I couldn't get to church, I watched
televangelists. Oral Roberts was my TV preacher of choice. I even
remember stuffing a few dollars in an envelope once—God only
knows where I managed to find the cash—and sending it in the

mail with my prayer requests. Oral Roberts himself had assured me, through my television screen, that he had a prayer team standing by, ready to read viewer requests—my requests. And not long after I sent that letter, I received a copy of Roberts' book, *Seed Faith Scriptures*. Whenever I was going through a tough time, as teenagers frequently do, I clung to that book. I saw in it the assurance that the God I professed to believe in really existed, and He was there, ready to help even me.

Ministers of any faith have far more power than they might imagine, especially those who broadcast over a universal medium such as television. Although healthy-minded people attend religious services, these gatherings also draw hurting, vulnerable individuals looking for hope. I now wonder how many 13-year-olds, desperate for feelings of comfort and safety; seniors; and sick, lonely or destitute people sent the few dollars they had to someone like Oral Roberts.

As with any association, an organization the size of Oral Roberts Ministries is bound to have its fair share of scandal or innuendo. Viewers couldn't help but see that, over the years, Roberts had acquired some pretty bold pieces of jewellery, and his suits weren't too shabby, either. People notice these kinds of thing, especially with someone as powerful as Roberts. According to one source, the only televangelist more popular than the Tulsa, Oklahoma, preacher was Billy Graham, who avoided scandal by being so sensitive about his position and appearances that he made it a priority to accept a smaller salary than other televangelists.

But televangelists are like infomercials—they are everywhere. And, like infomercials, they represent a buyer-beware situation. Some televangelists aren't at all what they seem. Although charming and charismatic, some of these preachers don't always live by the words they speak—or the truths they profess to read from scripture. And, though some might stretch what's morally or legally acceptable from time to time, others are downright criminal in their actions.

Such was the case of James Orsen Bakker, more popularly known as Jimmy Bakker. Bakker had been involved in several ministries with his wife, Tammy Faye, since 1966. Although many of the shows they initially worked on reached relatively small audiences by television standards, the Bakkers had a spark to their delivery and attracted larger and larger crowds, who eventually followed them from other people's shows to their own.

In 1975, the couple began the PTL Club (an acronym for Praise the Lord). Bakker's ministry grew, and millions of dollars poured in to support its efforts, thanks in part to Bakker's preaching that God is anxious to give his chosen people all their material desires—those chosen people, at least, in part, appeared to refer to the Bakkers—and that God rewards people who give in faith with more material wealth than they could ever imagine. However, it wasn't long before Bakker's façade as a man who did everything for the glory of God began to unravel. Allegations of Bakker's extramarital affair with Jessica Hahn, along with accusations of "homosexual encounters," added to the shock his followers felt when they learned that their favourite preacher was in trouble with the law.

In 1989, Jimmy Bakker was found guilty on 24 charges, ranging from mail fraud and wire fraud to conspiracy. In layman's terms, Bakker had been skimming the books to the tune of several million dollars. When the dust settled, Bakker spent a mere five years of his 45-year sentence behind bars. He hasn't gotten off so easy, as far as the government goes—he still owes them a whopping $6 million, according to one source.

Bakker's story isn't the only example of a body of believers who were promised material blessings if they sent money to support a ministry. Charlatan preachers have also promised their followers that if they give a certain amount of money to their ministry, a miracle will happen in their lives. "God multiplies the seed you sow, the supernatural power of God hits after you sow, not before, after," one popular televangelist told his audience in 1996.

Sometimes, the abuse of religion is far more subtle and not necessarily perpetrated by a religious leader. Access to potential victims through a mutual association with a church, synagogue or mosque is the method of choice for some con artists, who use this common ground to gain and exploit a victim's confidence. And the only thing these fraudsters are interested in is gaining access to their victim's money.

Such was the case of Salim Mohammed Damji.

WHERE IT ALL STARTED

The city of Toronto calls itself the cultural, entertainment and financial capital in Canada. Located near the north-western corner of Lake Ontario, Toronto is a place that attracts an eclectic assortment of people: the young, the business-savvy, artists and musicians and, of course, lake lovers.

Toronto was a place Salim Mohammed Damji loved to call home. In August 2000, the attractive 30-year-old had no reason to expect anything but bliss and excitement in his future. He had a lovely woman at his side, and the couple were planning their wedding. Even money didn't seem to be an obstacle. In fact, Lady Luck seemed to be shining on Damji quite extraordinarily. In an interview with CTV's *W-FIVE,* Damji said he'd won a staggering $800,000 playing Ontario's Pro-Line Sports Lottery. Most would consider the money a great start for a couple about to be married, but Damji had other plans for it.

Thinking of the years ahead, Damji thought the $800,000 represented a chance to invest in something that would continue to grow and offer the couple an ongoing income. While flipping through TV channels one day, Damji came across the Shopping Channel, which was advertising Instant White, a new tooth-whitening product. "What a great investment idea," he thought. "After all, doesn't everyone want to look great?" Reflecting on the workplace alone, where a person's appearance can make the difference between landing the perfect job and staying on the assembly line, Damji saw the potential for success.

Buying into a product that promises a bright smile would be a fairly safe gamble in so many ways.

As Damji tells it, he flew to New York and tried unsuccessfully to buy rights in Instant White. Damji was never clear about why he failed to acquire the rights, but apparently he continued to look for investment opportunities, his search eventually taking him to Miami. He later said that it was in Miami that he'd met the "questionable individuals" who would, from then on, make his life a living hell.

When he returned to Toronto, still without a clear idea of how to invest his money, Damji says a man named Richard Dawson casually approached him at a restaurant, and the two began talking about Instant White. Somehow, the meeting devolved into what Damji called direct threats by Dawson against Damji's fiancée and other family members. Damji said the man even had a picture of his fiancée and that he had no choice but to be drawn into what he described as a dark underworld of activity. His great descent began when these alleged underworld figures forced him to deliver packages of money around Toronto—his money, according to Damji.

"I could go to the police....But I thought, money is not as important as the lives of the people I love," Damji told *W-FIVE.* "So I said, 'Okay, fine.'"

Damji said these same culprits forced him into developing the Instant White investment scheme, instructing him to establish a company called Strategic Trading Systems (STS) and dictating how he should spend the more than $75 million he was supposed to have swindled from the thousands of trusting investors from Toronto and around the world. Damji explained that some of the money was earmarked for establishing his image: he lived a life of luxury that included a waterfront condo in Toronto worth $800,000; nine cars, including an assortment of Mercedes and BMWs; and ownership of a strip mall. Damji said that, aside from establishing his image, these dark influences in his life wanted him to look the part of a wealthy man, so that if authorities ever caught on to the fraud, they'd follow the money to Damji, and his criminal associates would never be identified. The rest of the money, millions of dollars of it, was shipped, as he was instructed to by these supposed puppeteers who were orchestrating his every move, to Internet gambling sites in Jamaica and Costa Rica.

And where did he get his victims? Why from his faith community, of course.

You Can Lead a Horse to Water *and* Make Him Drink

Although it's difficult to know the exact number of Ismailis living in Canada, it's estimated that the branch of the Muslim faith has roughly 90,000 followers. In 2006, an estimated 35,000 Ismailis lived in or around Toronto. It was into this community that, as the warmth of a hot summer began to wane and the cool breezes off Lake Ontario spelled the coming fall, Damji first presented his "investment opportunity."

Damji started by telling his friends and family members and fellow worshipers about Instant White. As he boasted about the benefits of the product and its ease of use, he also divulged that the Colgate-Palmolive Corporation was interested in the product Damji had supposedly patented and to which he allegedly owned the rights. The pharmaceutical company was, according to Damji, so interested in Instant White that they'd promised to buy it for a staggering $400 million. Those interested in buying in could receive as much as a 20-to-one profit—a $20 return for a single dollar investment. To add a little credence to his proposal, Damji said he'd donate $1.5 million to the Aga Khan Foundation over a five-year period—the Aga Khan is the imam or spiritual leader of the Ismailis, and the foundation formed in his name is a nonprofit international agency whose mandate, according to its Canadian website, is to support social development programs in Asia and Africa. Interestingly enough, this is one commitment on which Damji did follow through.

As a confidence man, Damji was scoring high marks. Those he approached found him personable, enthralled by the endless business possibilities he could foresee with his exciting new product, and he appeared to be generous with his money. He looked reputable, sincere and trustworthy in every way. In short, everything he did made him believable.

Interested investors hung on his every word. And they started digging into their wallets.

GROWING THE IDEA

They came out of the woodwork, it seemed, investing everything from a few hundred to many thousands of dollars. "I put in $20,000, but my whole family put in $100,000," an anonymous investor told Jonathan Jenkins of the *Toronto Sun,* describing how those who bought into the company were told to keep the investment quiet—the fewer the people who knew about it, the better potential return. Also, if Colgate caught wind of the publicity, the corporation might back out of the deal, which would be bad for everyone, Damji said. People trusted Damji so much that some of them borrowed money against their homes so they could invest in Instant White. Even the poorest of his acquaintances often begged Damji to make an investment for them.

"Damji, Damji," some of the elderly and poor attending prayers at the mosque Damji attended would call. "Damji, here—take. It's not much. Please." And Damji would find $100, $50 stuffed into the palm of his hand. He'd give them a reassuring smile, slip the cash into his pocket and promise to add another $100, another $50, and double their investment.

Even Damji's wife, Zara, got into the swing of things, selling stock options to support her husband's business. In her defence, she also claimed she was forced into cooperating, not by unnamed underworld figures but by a husband she trusted and tried to support. She wanted to be a good wife, and, now, all she had to show for her efforts were financial ruin and the loss of respect from those she loved. "My family, my parents, my brother, my friends, and my co-workers have lost a lot of money," she told *W-FIVE*. "They all invested."

Although several reports have Damji asking investors to keep quiet about their involvement with Instant White and STS, other news stories suggest Damji didn't shy away from promoting Instant White publicly. He presented the product at trade shows and told those who stopped by his booth about "Colgate's interest in the product." At different times during his two-year scam, Damji even posed as a dentist, making it even more believable that he could have developed and patented a tooth-whitening product. And yet, moments after sharing the information, he would ask the people he spoke with to keep it to themselves.

Of course, the scheme didn't make sense: if people really thought about what he was saying, they might have refrained from investing. That's exactly what one man, who asked not to be named, told the *Toronto Sun:* "It's like the Nigerian scam, greed over common sense." But Damji's long-winded speeches and charismatic ways were only part of his ploy to gain the confidence of his victims. By sharing everything he had on Instant White and then asking his investors not to share that information with others, he was demonstrating that he trusted them.

He was doing more than just promising a great return on the dollar; he was treating his investors like peers. How can you not trust someone who has demonstrated his trust in you?

To be fair, the Ismaili community is a closely knit group. Ismaili businesspeople tend to work together, getting tips and leads from one another and other members of their faith community. It wasn't uncommon to work this way. Concerns over Damji's business transactions arose when investors were promised payouts on certain dates and the payouts never materialized. Expected pay dates came and went without any word, and, when investors started calling Damji for updates and even, on some occasions, for their money back, he didn't answer their calls. Eventually, Colgate did learn about the story and denied having any involvement with Damji or plans to buy Instant White. The public was also discovering that Damji didn't own Instant White, nor did he hold a patent for it. Mild concern grew into panic, and then anger, as investors started to realize they'd been duped.

The Buck Stops Here

In April 2002, almost two years after Damji first started selling phony stocks in a company that didn't exist, he was arrested in a suspected "investment fraud scam." Angry investors crowded into a Toronto courtroom as a confused Damji couldn't remember his lawyer's name, and the judge was forced to adjourn the proceedings until the accused could acquire adequate legal representation.

As police were building their case against Damji, and even looking into the possibility that some of his fraudulent moneymaking schemes had ties to terrorist activities, the shady characters Damji claimed to be involved with and who allegedly forced him into his life of crime were never officially identified. In his report, Toronto lawyer and interim receiver John J. Chapman said, "(we) have been unable to independently verify any of Damji's allegations that he was the victim of an extortion plot and, indeed, many items alleged by Damji are inconsistent with other facts."

While Damji's case was developing, the investigation was also taking on a secondary focus. Police were asking anyone who'd done business with Damji or STS to come forward. Dozens of people crowded into the courthouse whenever Damji was scheduled to appear, but police suspected that there were far more victims than even some of their generous estimates might suggest. And, though many investors lost large amounts of money, one victim told police he lost an unbelievable $1.2 million with STS.

More and more victims came forward, and, by the end of the investigation, police estimated that as many as 6000 people had been conned by Damji. That number far exceeded Damji's carefully worded statement to the courts about taking "$41.7 million from nearly a thousand investors, over a two-year period." Although many of those investors were members of Ismaili communities in Toronto, Vancouver and Calgary, Damji's scheme targeted victims around the world.

It wasn't just the number of investors that continued to climb. The money Damji collected increased exponentially. By May 2002, the original estimates charging Damji's take at somewhere around $40 million had more than doubled. Investigators were now suggesting that the amount of cash that had been swindled was likely closer to $100 million. The now-infamous Instant White scam was being touted as one of the largest frauds ever perpetrated in Canadian history.

But where had all the money gone?

Problems in Paradise

Anyone who knew Damji knew that he lived an extravagant lifestyle. His friends, family and business partners took him at face value, believing he'd made good on his patented tooth-whitening product and was reaping the rewards of that investment. But, as the public learned exactly how much money Damji was thought to have swindled, they began to ask the inevitable question: if STS and Instant White were nothing more than a scam, where had Damji put the tens of millions of dollars he'd swindled?

"We don't know where any of the money went," Detective Constable Rodger Robertson told *Sun* reporter Tom Godfrey. "Some of it may have gone to terrorism. We don't know."

Others suggested that some of the cash was likely deposited in offshore accounts. The idea was shocking but not as alarming as the suggestion that Damji had problems with gambling. Damji admitted to losing $50 million to a Costa Rican bookie named Maynard Garber. If the money did make it to Garber, it suggested that the two men might have had some kind of arrangement to stash the money for later use. If, however, gambling was indeed behind the loss of money, as Damji claimed, the scenario was beyond belief. As Toronto lawyer Chapman said in his report, "the huge volume of losses alleged over 16 months equates to average losses of about $100,000 per day....It seems inconceivable...that Garber could not have had some concerns as to the source of Damji's funds or, alternatively, not had a suspicion that Damji had a serious gambling problem."

When the topic arose of where these millions had gone, Zara Damji was quick to chime in from the sidelines, saying she didn't believe all the money her husband was supposed to have scammed from unsuspecting investors had disappeared. She didn't believe in the gambling scenario, either. "If you're smart enough to do this, I don't think you're dumb enough to lose it all," she told *W-FIVE*.

Even without a clear understanding of what became of investor money, the law was tightening the noose around Damji. Damji was still trying to blame other people for his bad behaviour, and, despite attempts to get out of jail on bail, he spent the entire time between his initial arrest and subsequent sentencing hearing behind bars. Finally, on November 13, 2002, he pleaded guilty to "one count of fraud over $5000." To the thousands of people who'd lost millions because of Damji, the charge must have seemed a miscarriage of justice. By then, only a small amount of the money he'd swindled, about $350,000 from an Internet casino account, had been recovered. His property assets, which equalled roughly $4 million, were also seized. But the missing millions were still unaccounted for.

On November 15, a headline in the *Toronto Sun* read, "Report doubts fraud artist's plight tale 'inconsistent.'" According to the story, Damji wrote an apology to his victims but insisted that he, too, was a victim, repeating his earlier claims that he'd been forced into an extortion plot and that he'd lost millions of dollars gambling. Southam Newspapers reported that, at Damji's subsequent sentencing hearing, he said he was sorry, had begged for forgiveness from his victims and acknowledged that those he'd deceived wouldn't likely feel like forgiving him, in light of their loss. His greatest regret, he said, was losing the respect and trust he once had from his own community.

Crown prosecutor Alex Alvaro was as moved by Damji's words as his jilted investors were—which was not at all. Alvaro asked Justice Paul Bentley for a six-year sentence, plus time served. "No other case (in Canada) involves such a high number of individuals and such a high amount of loss," Alvaro told the court.

Justice Bentley obviously agreed with Alvaro's assessment of the situation and, on November 29, 2002, he slammed Damji with a sentence of six years and three months, telling him, "Your selfishness and callousness have devastated the lives of so many...This was a premeditated deception of grandiose proportions...The picture you present is of an incredibly greedy, materialistic individual."

Although Damji's sentence mildly placated some of his victims, others would have preferred a much stiffer sentence: because he hadn't perpetrated an act of violence during his criminal enterprise, with good behaviour, Damji could be out on parole in a year.

And that's pretty much what happened.

ANOTHER ROUND?

Damji was first paroled on November 9, 2004, and appeared to fly under the radar for a few months. He still insisted that his life was in danger in Toronto, so authorities relocated him to Ottawa. He landed an apartment on Stirling Avenue, living there under the guise of being a law student. He stayed for two months before ditching out on his new land-lady. She heard nothing of him until he was back in the news.

On Tuesday, May 24, 2005, the Instant White fraudster incited the wrath of his parole officer and was arrested and once again thrust into the public spotlight. This time, he was booked into the Ottawa-Charleton Detention Centre for a period of 30 days, until Repeat Offender Parole Enforcement officers decided whether to revoke his parole.

The news made headlines across the province, but officials were strangely silent on the reason for Damji's re-arrest. The *Ottawa Sun* reported obtaining parole documents highlighting some of the conditions of Damji's parole—one required Damji to report any and all of his financial transactions. The parole board also commented on their concern over Damji's risk to reoffend, saying they believed it was "significant," and that his "well-honed deception skills" were just one of the reasons for their concern.

After a couple of news reports, Damji again fell off the public's radar. It wasn't until April 2007, when a story about the con man landed in the pages of the *Toronto Star*, that people learned that Damji had been out on parole several times but had returned to jail just as frequently for various parole violations. In April 2007, Damji was making his way back into Toronto's Don Jail on "one count of fraud over $5000, uttering a forged document and conspiracy to commit an indictable offence for allegedly arranging [the] deposit of a stolen cheque made out for $8000 into someone's bank account." The tiger certainly hadn't changed his stripes, as arresting detective Jeff Thomson remarked to the media, but a scam for such a paltry sum of money did refocus the investigation on the possibility that Damji might not have the missing millions from his earlier scam safely stashed away, after all.

The next time Damji made headlines was on March 19, 2008. This time, his story of fraud and deception made it into the *National Post*. It described the actions of a large contingent of Toronto's Ismaili community, which was facing off against the Bank of Montreal (BOM), accusing the bank of turning a blind eye to Damji's activities. Banks typically question large deposits and withdrawals, and the BOM appeared to have overlooked this in Damji's case. The investors wanted to file a class-action lawsuit for $55 million in damages. No doubt, this would be but one of many lawsuits brought against Damji, every battle bringing with it a new set of angry victims. Although the full term of Damji's prison sentence expired on February 28, 2008, it's likely he will be haunted for life by the actions of his impulsive and greedy youth.

As of this writing, the latest action filed against Damji was in the Ontario Superior Court of Justice in August 2009. The suit represents an effort by the Interim Receiver to acquire money Damji allegedly had control over, to repay some of the investor loss under a Debtor Agreement that would see Damji retaining a percentage of the money. At that point, it was determined that there were "$78 million of losses attributable to the fraud by Damji and millions of dollars of that amount have not yet been specifically traced." However, the Interim Receiver did reveal that "Damji had control over in excess of $15 million derived from Damji's fraud and relating to investments made by Damji, and that these funds were not part of the funds subject to the agreement with Garber." In other words, there was money there, after all.

Although sympathetic to the efforts of the Interim Receiver and the desire to return investor money, Justice Nancy J. Spies refused to make the Order and dismissed the motion, explaining that, were she to make the Order, it would in effect "absolve Damji of his contempt and further reward him financially if he decides to comply with that Order." She called the Debtor Agreement "offensive" and that making the kind of Order suggested would set a dangerous precedent, potentially encouraging other con artists and fraudsters to dismiss the authority of the court and use what could be seen as the resulting loophole to benefit from their crimes. Justice Spies further challenged Damji and his legal representatives, demanding Damji divulge the whereabouts of any money he might still have tucked away—some sources suggested the hidden nest egg could be as much as $15 million—and if Damji didn't come clean on this information, he'd find himself behind bars once again.

Clearly, the victims of Instant White, and the Canadian public in general, have not heard the last word on Salim Mohammed Damji.

GOD'S FRAUD SQUAD

Although it might seem incomprehensible that con artists would exploit people of their own faith or ethnicity or vulnerable groups such as seniors, Damji's actions aren't unique to him. Governing bodies, such as the British Columbia Securities Commission (BCSC), refer to this kind of specialized targeting as "affinity fraud," and they've designated a team to combat the threat, calling it "God's Fraud Squad."

According to a *Globe and Mail* article penned by Patrick White, one in every 20 Canadians has been scammed by some kind of investment fraud. Affinity fraud represents the most difficult case to crack. "There's a real reluctance to report fraud within the religious community," Wayne Redwick, BCSC director of education initiatives, told White. "There's no way a government organization like ours can get access to various churches."

But God's Fraud Squad can. Since 2003, Father Seamus Mackrell, a Catholic priest, and Reverend John Hacock, a Presbyterian minister, have travelled to churches throughout BC's Lower Mainland and even as far away as New Mexico, educating congregations on how to identify affinity fraud within their own communities and what to do about it when they see it.

There is abundant evidence of the need for such a team. Following are just two of the cases in which the churches involved could have used the information provided by God's Fraud Squad to save their members from a lot of pain and suffering.

A HEART FOR THE UNDERPRIVILEGED?

Early in 2000, Reverend Narvin Wray Clarence Edwardson, a 68-year-old man who claimed to be a preacher and the moderator of the Baptist Church in Southeast Asia, was rapidly losing his cover. For a number of years, he'd been bilking people out of millions of dollars during his visits to churches throughout Canada and the U.S., asking for support for his rice-growing projects and orphanage- and hospital-building programs in Singapore, Manila and whatever parts of Asia tickled his fancy at any given time. He had a strange way about him—eccentric, some might say. Yet even his colleagues found him mesmerizing.

While at the pulpit, he'd talk about the orphans. He'd talk about the sick with no medical care to ease their pain. He'd suddenly burst into song, bellowing out an old, favourite hymn. On occasion, while standing before his congregation, he'd start talking about an investment opportunity he just had to share. Like Damji, Edwardson scammed his followers, and numerous colleagues within the larger Christian community, of their money by having them invest in products such as his Universal Diesel Liquefier. Tom Johnson, a Kelowna evangelical and retired ATCO Company employee, told Douglas Todd of the *Vancouver Sun* in 2000 that he'd invested $400,000 in luxury cars through Edwardson. When Edwardson learned that Johnson was trying to track him down and was digging into some of the preacher's other schemes, Edwardson responded by getting his family out of town and sending Johnson a fax. Johnson shared that fax with the *Sun*: "I am truly a Christian and under God's promise…No weapons formed against me can prosper [because] I put my full trust in Him." Clearly Edwardson believed his own rhetoric.

Johnson disagreed. "I've been devastated by this. I don't have much left. I don't even own my own car anymore…But I want to see justice done. This man is very persuasive. He's slick, professional and shrewd. He prays and sings and tells you how rich he is. And the key he uses to open doors is Christianity."

In 2004, Honourable Judge G.G. Sinclair of the Provincial Court of British Columbia found Edwardson guilty of several charges pertaining to claims made by just two of his many investors, for a total of almost $400,000. Edwardson was sentenced to 12 months of prison time for two of the charges and six months for the other two, with the sentences to run concurrently. In his reasoning, Judge Sinclair noted that, for the purposes of that particular set of proceedings, Edwardson had not been charged with fraud. But the result was clearly the same, as far as his victims were concerned.

Incidentally, when reporters looked for commentary from Edwardson's church, they were unable to find such an entity. Edwardson had apparently developed his own denomination as part of his guise; having a Filipino wife added some measure of credibility to his story.

An Open Door to Investments

Scamming the people who believed in you was something Gary McNaughton was also good at.

The Canadian-born church leader had moved around a bit before settling down in Elyria, Ohio, and taking on the role of youth assistant at the Church of the Open Door. His personable manner quickly gained him the respect of his peers. The vibrant gentleman also impressed the members of the church he served. For their loyalties, he offered to share with them his other love—investments. In partnership with his Canadian friend, Andrew K. Lech, McNaughton offered his colleagues and parishioners, about 150 of them altogether, a chance to invest in unregistered securities "in the form of notes [he] issued under the name of The Haven Equity Company (Haven Equity)." Investors were promised annual returns of somewhere between 15 and 35 percent, and, better still, that money would come to them in "monthly 'interest payments.'"

According to court documents, McNaughton sent the money to Lech, who, in turn, used his knowledge and trading contacts to produce the promised monetary gain. Money continued to come in, and, now and then, an investor would receive a cheque—just enough payback to soothe investors' doubts over slower-than-promised returns.

Sarah Presnell believed McNaughton's false promises and invested money with him. She was ill and wanted to make sure that her elderly husband and 56-year-old disabled daughter were well provided for, should she happen to pass on. So she drained the family bank account, even adding some of her daughter's savings to the pot, and came up with $25,000. McNaughton took the money, promising a $250 payout the following month. Presnell was no doubt relieved when that first payment came in. But when no further cheques followed, she started to panic. That money represented everything she and her family had. Losing it meant that the Presnells would be forced to sell their home and that their daughter wouldn't get the medical care she needed.

In the end, Presnell discovered she was more than justified in her concerns. By the time the law caught up with McNaughton and Lech, the pair had pulled in a lot of cash. Other investors were also starting to question things. And on June 23, 2003, McNaughton found himself facing an official complaint filed by the U.S. Securities and Exchange Commission, along with a "temporary restraining order and asset freeze." That action was followed up by two other Orders, one seeking a permanent injunction against McNaughton on December 4, 2003, and another action, "a Final Judgment and Order of Disgorgement" on August 23, 2004.

Coming up against the U.S. Securities and Exchange Commission appears to have been sufficiently disconcerting to McNaughton because, on March 5, 2007, he pleaded guilty to "10 counts of securities fraud, unlawful sale of unregistered securities, mail fraud and attempted tax evasion...The charges stemmed from McNaughton's role in (what amounted to) a Ponzi scheme in which he fraudulently raised at least $17 million from approximately 200 investors and which was the subject of a prior Commission action." McNaughton perpetrated his frauds between 1999 and 2003.

Despite the fact that the Church of the Open Door never invested with McNaughton and Haven Equity, some duped parishioners felt the church was at least partly liable. Pastor David Walls and other leaders in the faith community had not only invested their own money with McNaughton, they had also encouraged some of their parishioners and friends to check out McNaughton's investment opportunities—sharing the good news, in a way. We all know about the road to Hell being paved with good intentions—it could be argued that these well-meaning folks had inadvertently assisted McNaughton in leading his victims to their financial demise.

Presnell was not alone in telling reporters that she'd never have invested her money if she thought the investment opportunity wasn't condoned by the church. One couple tried to sue the church; they lost but appealed the decision. Others, like Seth Stevens of Amherst, a man who lost an estimated $750,000, placed the blame for his misplaced trust on himself. Ultimately, the situation couldn't help but cause rifts in an otherwise healthy and loving parish.

AFTERTHOUGHT

There's a saying in the New Testament: "Watch out for false prophets. They come to you in sheep's clothing, but inwardly they are ferocious wolves." Unfortunately, it's a truth that's far too evident in all walks of faith.

As with any of life's challenges, there is something to be learned from Salim Mohammed Damji, Reverend Edwardson and Gary McNaughton. In our enthusiasm to follow the tenets of our faith and open our hearts to reach out to those in need, we must balance that love and charity with some deep introspection. Some call that common sense.

Others call that prayer.

Chapter Three

Smoke and Mirrors

RICHARD BRYAN MINARD,
A.K.A. BRYAN ALLEN RICHARDS

~

The fact I get up in the morning means I sin.

–Richard Minard, as Bryan Richards, Christian rock jock,
broadcasting in Terrace, BC

The day Richard Minard walked into the office of the
Smithers *Interior News* to introduce himself to the community and promote his newest business venture was
overcast. Clouds hung off the peaks of Hudson's Bay Mountain,
which towered over the town higher, it seemed, that day than it
had at any other time, effectively blocking the sun more than
usual, even for this northern community.

Smithers, located on Highway 16, is tucked away in the
Bulkley Valley of British Columbia at the halfway point between
the province's two "Princes"—Prince George and Prince Rupert.
It was September, and the lush vegetation that cloaked the
mountainous interior of Canada's westernmost province and
tempted outdoors enthusiasts with endless potential for fun

throughout the summer months was turning its usual fall colours. Orange and gold had already replaced the deep green leaves clothing the stands of aspen trees interspersed throughout the balsam, spruce and pine. Backyard tamaracks were dropping their needles, salmon fry were leaving the valley on their migratory journey to the ocean and the bears were starting to think about taking a long winter snooze. Soon, hikers and bikers and kayakers would pack up their summer gear in favour of snowboards and skis. But, for now, the last few warm days of summer competed with the constant cloud cover that made up much of the darker days of the coming winter, hiding a typically shy sun. The day I met Richard Minard, the clouds were winning.

I knew about the interview. My editor had told me of a new "preacher" in town, who was trying to establish a radio show for youth, one that would feature modern Christian music. My editor thought it would make an interesting story. So did I—until Minard walked in the door.

"Hi, my name is Bryan Richards," he said, thrusting out his hand and adding that he was a minister with the Assemblies of God. (Throughout our acquaintance, I only ever knew him as Bryan Richards.)

Minard towered a good foot taller than my five-foot-four-inches. He was a muscle-bound, large-framed man, and I could see his pulse beating in the veins of his thick neck. That, coupled with the bulky sweatpants and T-shirt he wore, emblazoned with a sports logo that didn't make it into my long-term memory, cemented my first impression of the guy: this man wanted the world to know that he worked out regularly; no one could push him around.

Minard's dense, curly, shoulder-length hair plainly suggested that the man, already into his 40s, wouldn't have to worry about buying Rogaine any time soon. He wore a short beard and 'stash and apparently never took off the granny sunglasses he wore tight to the bridge of his nose. To me, he looked more like a poker player protecting his hand than a transparent man of God.

"Hello," I said as I gripped his hand hard and gave it a firm shake. "I was once married to a minister. And I don't trust you, either."

My response was so uncharacteristic and unbecoming of a supposedly unbiased news reporter that I startled myself as well as the colleagues who'd overheard me. Minard just laughed. Said we'd have to talk about that some day. Meanwhile, he had this radio show to tell me about.

And so it was that I came to pen the first story about Minard in the *Interior News,* promoting his efforts, when all the while I was suspicious of the man for no apparent good reason other than, as one individual put it to me, my own sour grapes.

An Ill Wind

Minard moved to Canada from the U.S., arriving in the Bulkley Valley in May 1999, supposedly on the heels of a ladylove he'd met on a Christian Internet dating site and had planned to marry. But a number of women popped in and out of Minard's life during his time in the valley, suggesting that this relationship must either have fizzled by September or was coming to an end when his first story hit the papers, because it wasn't something he discussed when explaining his move to northern BC.

He did discuss his appearance and approach, explaining that the casual clothing, dark glasses and laid-back style put people at ease. He wanted to replace what some suggested were traditional, hierarchical barriers between ministers and laypeople with a simplicity and straightforwardness that would attract a wider demographic. He hoped his sociable, friendly manner would attract unchurched youth; he wanted them to see that they could be cool and a Christian.

Over a dozen or so weeks, Minard travelled the two hours between Smithers and Terrace to produce his Christian radio shows, which were geared to attract that younger crowd and replace the sometimes-negative messages they received through secular rock and pop music with the hopeful message of the Gospel. Assisted by engineer Chris Andrews, of Skeena Digital Recording in Terrace, Minard produced one selection of half-hour segments with Christian pop and country music for valley listeners tuned in to Terrace radio station CJFW and another assortment of shows with a hard rock edge that he claimed was for KKLA, a radio station in Los Angeles.

The Christian Power Hour, as Minard called the show that some critics said was not as much a sign of poetic license as it was of his underlying dishonesty, aired on CJFW from 6:30 to 7:00 PM every Sunday. That Minard's brainchild was sandwiched between the popular, internationally syndicated Christian serials *Odyssey* and *Focus on the Family* gave the "cool preacher" and his program a great deal of credibility in the minds of his listeners. In reality, Minard didn't need a lot of faith to believe that his future offered nothing but promise.

To his credit, the self-proclaimed minister took his time creating an interesting format for his young audience. Minard typically decided on a theme for each program, chose his songs so their messages reinforced each other and seamlessly wove scripture, accompanied by his own unique commentary, throughout each segment. Claiming to have 18 years of experience in the Christian music industry in the U.S. during the 1980s and 1990s as the host of a syndicated show that aired on more than 200 radio stations and targeted the college market, Minard was well equipped to the task.

Even though I never saw his eyes—his sunglasses stayed on throughout the entire interview and were on every time I bumped into him in the relatively small town of Smithers—it was hard to argue with his apparent sincerity. According to Minard, who said he'd spent several years working with Chuck Colson's prison ministry and Promise Keepers, an organization promoting family values, producing his shows would cost about $2000 a month, which he intended to pay out of his own pocket. After all, his motivation in this particular endeavour, as it was with Colson and Promise Keepers, was to spread the message of Christ, not to make a living from his efforts. Of course, he'd certainly entertain receiving donations from Christian businesses interested in sponsoring his efforts; in fact, he canvassed for them. It was an easy sell in a community of Christian business owners with children or grandchildren they worried about, and the more money he brought in, the more airtime he could purchase and the wider an audience he could reach. The opportunities were limitless; the world was his stage.

But where did Minard get the money he needed for his initial investment in the *Christian Power Hour*? He didn't dress in designer sweats, didn't carry himself in a way that suggested he was flush financially; he did like to play the part of a wealthy man by claiming to have a Lexus and Mercedes back in Los Angeles, but valley folks never witnessed this supposed wealth. And the cost of running his program was more than an old newspaper hack like myself earned in a month. So where was all this money coming from?

Enter the small, out-of-the-way community of Granisle.

A Good Eye

The village of Granisle first took shape at the end of a rough and winding secondary highway along the shores of Babine

Lake in the 1960s. The long, thin body of water, some 170 kilometres in length, had already gained notoriety as the province's longest natural lake, and the area was becoming known for its copper mines. In 1971, the partial skeleton of a Columbian mammoth, dating back about 34,000 years, was uncovered by workers excavating the nearby open-pit Bell Mine site, giving yet another boost to the growing town's budding notoriety.

But there was much more to this remote location than precious minerals and archaeologically significant skeletons and petroglyphs.

The Carrier people, the area's first inhabitants, already knew of Babine Lake's natural beauty and abundant fish and wildlife, and it wasn't long after the new settlement established itself that its non-native residents also gained an appreciation for their new home's natural wealth. Although Granisle experienced a period of boom, becoming home to as many as 3000 residents during its heyday, it wasn't long before the valuable minerals being mined there were harvested and the veins dried up. Without a mining industry to supplement the area's logging industry, jobs became scarce. Folks slowly migrated to other communities—communities such as Houston, 70 kilometres south, with its lumber mills and better roads and mini shopping mall. Only about 400 people call Granisle home today; not much has changed since 1999. But when Minard happened on the village, he couldn't help but notice that there was still something of value to be mined there.

Exactly how the American-born transplant discovered this hidden jewel in the British Columbia wilderness isn't clear. Perhaps it was his innate knack for honing in on business opportunities he knew he could sell to unsuspecting Christians—in this case, Christians with a penchant for the outdoors—that first drew him to this remote environment. Perhaps he was just curious and, in what was later described as his attempt to evade U.S. authorities by fleeing to Canada, he took a little side trip on his way to Smithers. Either way, Minard knew a gem when he saw it.

During its days as a busy quarry town with a bright future, Granisle had developed several amenities. Among them were a couple of two-storey motels with kitchenette-equipped rooms and an assortment of rustic cabins that visitors often rented. Many of these units overlooked the lake, and, after a busy day, guests found it pure heaven to sit back and gaze across the water.

Of course, with Granisle's decline, the motels and cabins were no longer full of visitors or prospectors or businessmen meeting with mining managers. In fact, except for the occasional hockey tournament and a few adventurous retirees who found peace and tranquility in the small community, the town was mostly empty. A sad waste of resources, Minard must have thought, what with all those fish and a wilderness teeming with wild game. He knew that outdoorsmen in the U.S. would jump at the chance to spend two weeks in these woods. Perhaps this was how Minard came up with the scam that would eventually land him in court and find him making a lot more enemies than friends.

I've Got This Land in Timbuktu

When Minard first spoke to me about the *Christian Power Hour,* he mentioned that his radio venture was partly funded by his business, Granisle Time Share Condos. He explained that he sold timeshares for a resort he was part owner of on Babine Lake. The resort, according to one source, was none other than the two-storey motel, which was partially on its way to being converted into condominiums and, according to other sources, included the rustic cabins. Whichever is true, Minard directed most of his advertising efforts toward American hunters, though he wasn't opposed to encouraging the odd local to invest in the resort as a vacation property. His dream was to eventually develop a sportsman's club in Granisle. And, really, anyone who'd ever visited the area would agree it wasn't such a bad idea.

On the website he created to publicize his perceived goldmine in northern BC, Minard highlighted the area's natural beauty, its lake and the streams packed with steelhead, sturgeon, trout and sockeye, pink and spring salmon. Big-game hunters would find the area rife with moose, deer, bears, mountain goats and sheep, he said. And those interested in hunting smaller species would find plenty of grouse. Later, when visitors had their fill of hunting, the wilderness surrounding Granisle offered endless opportunities for hiking, swimming, photography and just about any other creative interest they might have. There was no end to the bounty that visitors to Granisle could experience, and Minard didn't miss a beat when it came to promoting it all on his website.

Baiting his possible investors with glossy photographs and carefully worded descriptions, Minard finished the job of luring them in by inviting them to the resort on his coin, showing them around—within reason—and presenting them with an opportunity they couldn't refuse. For an incredibly reasonable price, Minard offered his prospective clients the opportunity of two weeks at the resort every year for life. All they had to do was sign this little contract and put down a fee of $5000 to $10,000. The price wasn't really exorbitant—if indeed Minard followed through with his promises.

A lot of people in the valley, as well as the potential customers he wooed elsewhere, initially bought into Minard's persona and suave manner and believed he was an innovative businessman. He won himself a lot of loyal fans through his radio show; the show gave folks something concrete to measure when making their assessment of the new man in town. He sounded like a guy who knew what he was doing and who really cared about spreading the Gospel message. He also quoted scripture at every opportunity—knowing your Bible buys a lot of brownie points for people whose Christian faith is central to their lives.

Enter an unnamed 23-year-old Smithers businessman. Eager to get in on the bottom rung of a new enterprise, the young man allegedly paid Minard $7000 for his timeshare condo. The would-be entrepreneur, who asked for anonymity in the media, told reporters from the *Vancouver Sun* that he was impressed with the condo Minard showed him and was dazzled by his charisma. "The fact he was a Christian was a clincher," the man said.

While a few locals were getting interested in Minard's resort proposal, interest was also growing from potential clients across the line. Michael Polito worked long, hard hours at Tri-Valley Construction, his industrial contracting business near San Francisco, California. In what little leisure time he had, Polito travelled to British Columbia to go fishing and hunting. When he saw the advertisement for Minard's Granisle Time Share Condos, Polito's interest was piqued. The ad directed Polito to a website with more information on the opportunity, affiliating it with Cross Net Marketing Group of Thousand Oaks, California. Polito later learned that Cross Net was yet another phony company established by the man he knew as Bryan Richards, but, at the time, everything seemed legitimate. If Polito bought a timeshare, he'd have his own getaway, and not breaking for a personal vacation every year would be tantamount to wasting money.

"Bryan explained how he was an owning partner in the Grande Isle Resort [sic] and said it was backed up by the British parliament or the government of Canada, [so] in the event it was to go bankrupt or cease to operate, we would all be covered in our investment," Polito told the *Vancouver Sun* in May 2000. "It sounded good to me, so I said: 'All right Bryan, what do I need to do here?'"

Without seeing the unit firsthand, Polito wired Minard a $6500 down payment on a $10,500 investment. A few months later, Minard called to ask if Polito was interested in investing in more timeshares; Minard suggested flipping them and splitting the profit. Polito told Brock Ketcham, a reporter who later penned an article for *Reader's Digest,* that Minard said, "We can make half a million dollars here." Although Polito still hadn't seen the property, he was interested enough to send another $25,000 to Minard in three instalments. Polito promised to pay the balance when he came north to see the resort. In the end, Polito paid Minard roughly $35,000 for seven timeshares—but he wasn't as sure of his investment when he finally made it to Granisle. What he saw was in stark contrast to the photographs Minard had posted on his website. Worse, his suspicions were being reinforced by those of another pair of investors.

Dan and Maureen Holbrook of Reno, Nevada, had also invested a considerable portion of their savings in Minard's time-share scheme. The couple, who also only knew Minard as Bryan Richards, parted with $6500 before arriving in Granisle. A couple of months after Polito's visit to Granisle, Dan Holbrook called Polito and asked about his interest in the resort. Holbrook shared his concerns about the timeshare project and told Polito that he'd done a little digging on the man whose signature appeared on the contract—Dan's only proof of purchase. Holbrook had asked a friend in law enforcement to run a check on Minard. "We could not find anything on Bryan Richards, and that really made the hair on the back of my neck stand up," Holbrook told the *Vancouver Sun*.

Polito still wanted to give Minard the benefit of the doubt, but two months had passed since Polito had handed Minard the balance of his payment for the extra timeshares, and Polito had yet to see any return on his investment. Whenever Polito asked about it, Minard quoted scripture and told Polito to trust him. Holbrook's phone call unsettled Polito, as did his comments that he'd been told Minard didn't actually own the resort in which he was selling his timeshares. Polito prided himself in being an astute businessman. Was it possible he'd been taken by a con man?

TIME TO ACT

By now, Polito was all out of Christian charity and was determined to find out everything he could about the man who'd swindled him. He decided to hire a detective and found one of the best hanging his shingle in Smithers.

Brian Dancey had retired from his duties as an Abbotsford police officer in 1979 and had spent the '80s working security at various gold mines. In 1990, he established a private detective business in Smithers. Anyone with a cursory experience of the small, touristy town might wonder at the need for such an enterprise there, but, over the years, Dancey kept himself busy and had built a solid practice. His many years of experience didn't go unnoticed by Polito. The contractor was grateful to acquire such a skilled detective who was also so well versed in the area.

Dancey didn't disappoint.

The detective began following Minard, often speaking with people seconds after Minard did. Dancey gathered information, took copious notes, dug into all the ins and outs of Minard's dealings and uncovered a whole lot more than problems with Minard's Granisle resort scheme. He discovered that a lot more people were suspicious of Minard's interactions than had let on—people such as Pastor Don Richmond, of Smithers' Mountain View Assembly.

THE LOCAL ANGEL

Minard began attending Mountain View Assembly on his arrival in the valley. At the time, he was dating Shelley Fisher, the woman he supposedly intended to marry. After first connecting online, Shelley and Minard met in person and spent some time in Vancouver; Minard then followed his new fiancée to her home in the Bulkley Valley. While there, Fisher agreed to let Minard live with her, a situation that didn't sit well with some of the church's religious leaders.

As a "man of the cloth," Minard was living a lifestyle that was far from meeting with the approval of Richmond and others in the church community. In Christian circles, a ceremony involving a ring and vows to God is supposed to occur before a man and a woman move in together, especially if one of them is an ordained minister.

And then there were those sunglasses: Minard didn't even take them off at church. And though his habit of inserting Bible passages into every conversation seemed endearing at first, over time, his words seemed forced, not at all sincere, leading some people to wonder if Minard was hiding something behind his well-crafted façade.

"He could talk the talk, and he always had some spiritual thing—spiritual-sounding thing to say, and that kind of made me a little uneasy because it didn't seem to fit," Pastor Richmond told *W-FIVE* in May 2001.

While Polito worked one angle, having Dancey collect information on Minard, Richmond began working another. He asked Minard for the membership card that would prove his alleged connection with the Assemblies of God. "I checked that out. And there was no record of anything to do with the Assemblies of God, which is a huge organization with lots of accountability, lots of standards, lots of checks and balances. He didn't check out," Richmond told reporters.

Richmond later met with Reverend Dwayne Goertzen of Smithers Evangelical Free Church, and the men tried to "clear the air" by meeting with Minard. Richmond told Ketcham that he asked the Smithers rock jock for one thing: "I have a card here...these are my credentials. Where are yours?" Minard asked for time, said he'd have to send away for his identification. Three weeks later, when he still couldn't produce the requested piece of paper, Richmond felt vindicated in his suspicions—he just knew Minard wasn't what and who he pretended to be.

When Minard's relationship with Fisher ended, Richmond had another reason to worry about Minard. He started courting the unmarried women of Richmond's parish—especially those who were vulnerable. "He was hitting on women, and I was concerned about his financial scams," Richmond told John Young of the *Interior News*. "I was on his tail because I felt he was harming the community. He was trying to get money from people, he was harming the Gospel..."

Richmond finally did something he'd never done before—he asked Minard to leave the parish. "I've never done this in all my 20 years of ministry, but I said to him that because of his activities he was not welcome."

FIGHTING BACK

By now, Minard's radio show had earned a loyal following, despite some concerns from a few now-vocal individuals.

Listeners were pleased with the *Christian Power Hour* and its format. The Christian business community must have been impressed, too, because some of them allegedly bought into the program with donations or through paid advertising. It was enough of a boost for Minard to start denouncing Richmond and his challenges to Minard's lifestyle, as well as the Ministerial in general. In November 1999, I wrote a follow-up piece to Minard's introductory story, highlighting how—according to Minard's testimony—the show was growing exponentially.

"In effect, the show has gone worldwide," Minard told me during that second interview for the *Interior News.* "Well, it will almost be worldwide, figuratively speaking, simply because the Internet is worldwide—it has no boundaries."

Minard explained that a partner in New Jersey was penetrating the European market, especially stations in Warsaw and Krakow in the partner's home country of Poland. "Anything that comes from here [North America], my people think it's gold," Andy Suzkis, Minard's American partner, told me during a telephone interview. According to Minard, CDs of the show were being made—he was targeting an initial run of 5000 copies. Although things appeared to be running like a well-oiled machine, the majority of the claims regarding the radio program were never verified.

To hear Minard tell it, life was good, but all was not exactly how he wanted it to be. He was unhappy about the lack of support he'd expected from religious leaders in the valley. In fact, he was being challenged directly by some members of the area's Ministerial, and this made him bristle. In his view, their criticism arose because Minard didn't "go through official church channels" to develop his ministry, and he saw these critics as "legalists." Some of the Ministerial went on record with the *Interior News,* countering Minard's assessment of their concerns. "We understand legalism as a system of rules necessary to earn salvation...the Bible does not teach this, and church history verifies the ineffectiveness of legalism. The Bible, however, does have standards for those in Christian ministry."

There it was, in black and white for anyone who cared to read; although no one was accusing of Minard of anything in particular, he was being challenged. It was clear that, to a few of his alleged colleagues, he wasn't measuring up to some of the standards set for Christian ministers.

If Minard was concerned by the public criticism, he didn't show it. In fact, he strutted through town looking more confident as the days wore on. He continued to claim the growth of his radio show, continued to accept donations and money for on-air advertising, continued to brag about his exploits. He also continued to promote his timeshare scheme.

THE DYNAMIC DUO

By now, Richmond and Dancey were aware of each other's interest in Minard and began sharing notes. Dancey discovered that the social insurance number Minard passed around didn't actually belong to him. Instead, it belonged to a child in the U.S. His Utah driver's licence and California birth certificate, both under the name of Bryan Allen Minard, also turned out to be fakes.

Dancey also discovered that Dan Holbrook, who'd contacted Polito some time earlier, was correct in his assumptions about the ownership of Granisle Time Share Condos. Minard was not part owner, as he claimed. In fact, Vancouver-area businessman Don Frederickson owned the property. And, though Minard did appear to have originally arranged to lease units for timesharing, the owners cancelled the option when Minard didn't follow through with the cash needed to back up his proposal. Apparently, Minard didn't let that little technicality get in the way of his own business aspirations, because he went ahead with his plans to sell timeshares, anyway. As Dancey later told the *Vancouver Sun,* "On Sundays [Minard] prayed on his knees, [and] on Mondays he preyed on his fellow man."

During his surveillance, Dancey saw Minard having coffee at Tim Hortons with a young dry-waller named Sean Westle. Dancey approached Westle on February 3, told Westle about the suspicions folks had about Minard and asked how he and Minard had become acquainted. Westle said that he and Minard shared a belief in God, but, more recently, Minard had tried to get Westle to sell timeshares in Minard's resort scheme; Westle wasn't interested.

The next day, Minard, who had become increasingly suspicious of everyone, made a strange phone call to Westle. Minard's house overlooked a church where Westle was doing some dry-walling. Minard thought he'd noticed a strange vehicle parked on the highway nearby and called Westle. Westle said he didn't know what Minard was talking about; he hadn't noticed anything. Shortly after the call, Minard came down to the church in person and had a tête-à-tête with Westle. He told Westle he was moving to Vancouver, that he needed to get away from what he said were false accusations by Polito and Holbrook. Once Minard left, Westle called Dancey with the news.

Richmond and Dancey went to the Smithers' RCMP with their suspicions and the evidence they'd gathered on the mystery man who'd invaded their peaceful town. By the time Corporal Pete Henzel pulled Minard in for questioning, more than a half a dozen formal complaints had been lodged against him.

Minard might have thought he could con an entire town and a pastor or two and handle himself with a backwoods cop, but he soon found he'd met his match in Smithers. Minard was arrested on February 5, 2000, getting his first taste of Canadian justice when officers locked his cell door just after midnight on February 6. The next day, Corporal Len Meilleur fingerprinted Minard and told him his prints were being sent to the FBI. After months of living a lie and claiming to be someone he wasn't, Minard had apparently had enough: his confidence deflated, the person everyone knew as Bryan Richards finally revealed his true identity.

UNMASKED

Bryan Allen Richards was actually Richard Bryan Minard, a con man from the U.S. with a long list of charges ranging from fraud and forgery to domestic assault. He was flown to Vancouver on February 8, 2000, and later driven to a jail in Washington state. From there, he was moved to Idaho, where he faced breach of probation charges. Surprisingly, to anyone who'd ever dealt with Minard in Canada, he was placed on probation.

Before his arrest, suspicious that law enforcement was on his tail, Minard tried to pull off one last swindle—he tried to cash a cheque from a Port Moody woman interested in buying into Granisle Time Share Condos. As serendipity would have it, the woman was a friend of Shelley Fisher, Minard's ex-fiancée. When Fisher found out, she alerted her friend to Minard's dubious behaviour, and the woman stopped payment on the cheque.

Minard needed money if he had any hope of escaping the authorities, and, in a last act of desperation, without an ounce of visible regret, Minard approached Bob and Diane Walker for help. Minard had befriended the couple soon after his move to Smithers, even spending Christmas with them, but he didn't let their friendship weigh on his conscience. Minard conned the Walkers, who operated a small business in Smithers, into cashing the cheque he knew was no good. It was his final scam before he planned to leave the valley, and all the people he'd swindled, forever.

Although the exact number of scams in which Richard Bryan Minard was allegedly involved is unknown, following are just a few of the enterprises he was believed to have established or had some connection with and that were reported in various media outlets:

Babine Lakes Vacation Club

Cross Net Marketing

Cross Net Marketing Group

Granisle Time Share Condos

Gold Links 2U Profit Share

Universal Millionaires Connection

Christian Power Hour Radio Network

Spirit Productions

The Fellowship of Christian Artists

The Christian Artists Fan Club

In a 2002 interview with *Reader's Digest,* Richard Bryan Minard continued to back what many called his less-than-honest claims by saying he never intended to harm anyone through any of his dealings—a little thing like selling something that wasn't his didn't appear to strike Minard as dishonest. Although, to anyone's knowledge, Minard has yet to produce a membership card for the Assemblies of God, he continued to stand by his claim that he attended a seminary and later took theological courses through correspondence. In his mind, at least, he was a minister. He also said he was a U.S. serviceman and maintained the truth behind the stories he told me about the years he spent working at radio stations in California and across the U.S.

The individuals named in this story represent only a handful of those who, over the years, were allegedly attracted by Minard's self-assured demeanour and promises of nirvana; there might have been others. These people trusted Minard, believed in his confident swagger, booming voice and big promises. They took him at his word, believing that the man of the cloth, as he claimed to be, would not be anything less than honest.

In November 1999, Minard told me that, in everything he did, he was true to himself and to what he perceived God wanted him to be. "That," he said, "was all that mattered." Even after being apprehended by RCMP, extradited to the U.S., facing his accusers on numerous occasions and found guilty of several offences, Minard stood firm in his skewed beliefs about himself. He told one reporter that he is what he is; any misconceptions are ours.

Idaho prosecuting attorney Richard Roats, in speaking with *Reader's Digest,* begged to differ. Roats went on record saying that Minard was well versed in his façade as a "charismatic man of the cloth," and was likely to continue targeting small communities where "law-enforcement resources are stretched... This guy is a menace to society."

For now, the voice of Richard Bryan Minard has been silenced. But for anyone who remembers the *Christian Power Hour* and knew the man personally, his end-of-show sign-off probably haunts them, just a little: "Hey, have a good one. And we'll see you next week—if the Lord doesn't come back first."

Chapter Four

Playing Like a Rockefeller—A Man of Great Expectations

CHRISTOPHE THIERRY DANIEL ROCANCOURT, A.K.A. CHRISTOPHER ROCKEFELLER ET AL

~

I would not consider myself a criminal—I steal with my
mind...if I take things, if that is your definition of
a criminal, then I am a criminal.

–Christophe Rocancourt, in conversation with reporters from
the *New York Times*

THE CANADIAN CONNECTION, PART I

In the neighbourhood of Oak Bay, a small community minutes outside of Victoria on BC's glorious Vancouver Island, the evening of Friday, April 27, 2001, was characteristically mild, compared to April weather in other parts of the country. By this time of year, avid gardeners were already gauging the risk of planting the first tomatoes outside, and outdoor enthusiasts were lacing up their jogging shoes or checking their bike tires before heading out on the trails. Perhaps it was to his detriment that Christophe Rocancourt hadn't caught spring fever—at least, not that day. He was at home, in a posh hotel, with his wife, Pia, and their son, Zeus, settling down for the night.

Acting on a tip from the RCMP's commercial crime squad, local police investigators surrounded Rocancourt's home. Did he sense anything untoward in the atmosphere? Or was he sitting comfortably with Zeus, reading him his favourite book? Was he watching the evening news? Cooking dinner with Pia? Whatever Rocancourt was up to, he probably wasn't expecting a face-to-face with the law.

The sharp knock at the door was probably the first clue that Rocancourt's visitor wasn't looking for pleasant chatter and a glass of wine. There's no place to run when you're in a hotel room, and so, with his characteristically charming demeanour, Rocancourt opened the door. Pia and Zeus, just steps away, looked on to see who'd popped by for a visit. And, although the family might have been surprised by the barrage of men and guns and the curt orders being barked at them, the arrest went smoothly.

The Mounties had just bagged an international criminal.

THE EARLY YEARS

According to most sources, the man who would eventually be known as the "Fake Rockefeller" was born Christophe

Thierry Daniel Rocancourt in Honfleur, France, on July 16, 1967. The small coastal town was a quaint corner of the world, to be sure, but Christophe's foundational years were memorable for all the wrong reasons. His mother, Annick Villers, was just 17 and a hardened prostitute when her first child was born. Christophe's father, Daniel Rocancourt, was a housepainter who found refuge from his dissatisfaction with life in alcohol. The two had wed in June 1967, but marriage hadn't changed their individual behaviours. Annick continued to ply her trade, and Daniel continued to drink. Before long, a daughter came along, yet Annick still worked as a prostitute. By now, her sister had joined her on the streets, and the children were often left unattended while their mother and auntie turned tricks.

Daniel became suspicious that Annick was not only selling sex but giving it away for free to another lover. Distressed over the possibility that his wife was having an affair, Daniel left. Annick took the two children to her parents' home and apparently left them there. Annick's parents, who were also impoverished and lived in squalid conditions, struggled to care for the youngsters, until Daniel returned from Belgium and reclaimed them. Although he didn't take up with Annick again, he did attempt to form a relationship with her sister. This also fizzled, as did another short-lived affair, prompting Daniel to decide that relinquishing Christophe and his sister might give him a better chance at developing a meaningful relationship. Besides, the children would be better off living elsewhere. So, he placed the children in an orphanage in Saint-Germain Village.

From the time he arrived at the orphanage in October 1976, to the day Daniel died in 1991, Rocancourt dreamed of being reunited with his father. But even if that dream was never realized, Rocancourt was a survivor. He was academically bright and, while in the orphanage, maintained good grades. He was also good at getting himself into hot water and even better at finagling his way out of it. "Whenever he got in trouble, he could charm his way out—always a bit of a talker, you know," Patrick Hnoy, Rocancourt's school counsellor, told *Vanity Fair*.

In 1979, things began to look up for the young orphan. Rocancourt, now 12 years old and a strapping young lad who showed a lot of potential, was adopted by a military man and his family living in Le Neubourg. Believing that a strict regime would straighten out the sometimes-wayward boy, Rocancourt's new father raised him with a heavy hand. The transition from a life with little to no parental involvement to one with a parent avidly engaged in the boy's upbringing must have been tough on Rocancourt. No one is certain of what happened next, but, by the time Rocancourt was in his teens, he was wandering the streets of Paris.

While in Paris, Rocancourt turned away from the family who'd tried to care for him during the last six years as well as the members of his birth family with whom he still communicated on occasion. In Paris, Rocancourt remade himself for the very first time. He was no longer Christophe Thierry Daniel Rocancourt, orphan boy and street roué—he was now a Russian nobleman. Of course, a young man with great expectations could not settle for being a count or baron; Rocancourt was a prince—Prince de Galitzine, though his thick French accent and lack of Russian likely didn't fool many people.

Rocancourt did, however, find himself in jail before too long. One source suggested he'd been locked up for "forgery, counterfeiting and petty larceny" several times between 1987 and 1992. And according to *Dateline,* Rocancourt made his first really big move when he was 23, forging "a deed for a Paris building he didn't own and then [selling] it" for $1.4 million. Although the scam got him into trouble, his charismatic ways, flashy smile and calm, lilting voice put others at ease and helped him regain his freedom.

Rocancourt's ruse as Prince de Galitzine must have been laughable to some and his additional alter egos annoying to others. But the sad reality was that this young lad, desperate for a home, a family and a sense of belonging, was re-creating not only himself but also his family of origin; he put himself in situations in which he loved himself and others made him feel loved and wanted. Living the script became a way of life, even if the entire experience was nothing more than an illusion. And the illusions changed repeatedly and rapidly. In his bold attempt to create that sense of belonging, Rocancourt changed his name the moment his current incarnation no longer served his purposes or when he got bored with it, and, with each successive re-creation, the lines between reality and fantasy became more and more blurred.

If Rocancourt's life of sham and deceit had merely focused on a need for love and acceptance, and his tendency to connect himself with people of authority was nothing more than a byproduct of his narcissist nature, one might turn a blind eye to his antics. But Rocancourt's charades were far more sinister. While still in Europe, he appeared to have accelerated rapidly from small-time thief to accomplished and dangerous criminal. Swiss police suspected Rocancourt of being one of three men who allegedly attacked and confined a woman in her home in Geneva, Switzerland, on September 15, 1991, before forcing her to help them rob the jewellery store in which she worked. The men were believed to have escaped with about $400,000 worth of merchandise.

The only glitch in the plan was the getaway, the thieves making their escape on foot, instead of zipping away in a getaway car. It would be many years before Rocancourt was extradited to Switzerland to face charges in the case, and, even then, without enough evidence to support their charges, the Swiss government was unable to convict him. Swiss authorities were taking no chances, however; they expelled Rocancourt from the country until 2016.

Immediately following the attack and robbery, Rocancourt left Europe and his former escapades behind, in favour of trying his hand in glitzy, star-studded Los Angeles, where he could make himself at home with the rich and famous. Initially, Rocancourt mingled with other French-speaking expatriates. Sometimes he'd use his real name, Christophe Rocancourt. But, over time, he branched out, assimilating himself into the Hollywood elite and taking other identities, such as Christopher De Laurentiis, supposed relative of film producer Dino De Laurentiis, or a relative of Sophia Loren or Oscar de la Renta. With each persona, the ruse was much the same: it was a game of "look at me, I'm rich and famous, just like you, so you can trust me." Perhaps it was the way he held himself, confident in every move he made, that quelled any doubts about his authenticity. He could speak the language of Versace and Prada, argue philosophy and was well read, capable of holding an intelligent conversation with almost anyone. He dedicated a great deal of time to rubbing shoulders with anyone he thought might buy his act. He was, in effect, building loyalties and collecting contacts. So charismatic was the poor orphan boy that, though some people might have raised their eyebrows at his gruff mannerisms, casual dress and baseball cap worn back to front, they never guessed the truth behind Rocancourt nor suspected he had anything sinister in his heart.

At least, not right away.

NEW WORLD METAMORPHOSIS

It was often unclear, even to the authorities, which alias Rocancourt used at any given time. But in June 1992, while attending Bar One, an elite nightspot in North Hollywood, Rocancourt spotted a lovely young woman working at the coat check. Gry Park was minding her own business, reading her Bible between customers and unaware that Rocancourt couldn't stop staring at her, until he begged for an introduction. The attraction was understandable. Gry was beautiful and had a kind, wholesome heart, to boot.

Rocancourt introduced himself to Gry as Christopher De Laurentiis, Hollywood film producer Dino De Laurentiis' nephew. He confessed to being smitten with her and, before long, that he wanted to marry her. Day after day, he sat by her side, quietly sometimes, and at other times trying to get Gry to talk. Although she wasn't a stranger to interest from men, no one had ever charmed Gry the way Rocancourt did. Eventually, he wore her down enough that she finally agreed to speak with him.

Talking was great for a while, but it wasn't enough to sustain Rocancourt's attention. He wanted more. He always wanted more. He persisted in getting to know her, opening up about himself—making himself vulnerable and sharing his personal struggles with others always made them feel safe. And it worked, too. Gry sensed a tone of desperation in the young man's words that touched her heart. Gry was also a giver. She believed the best of people and wanted to help whenever she saw a need.

Initially, Rocancourt put his best foot forward. He was a gentleman to her always. Even when Gry finally agreed to a Hawaiian getaway but insisted they stay in separate rooms, he didn't balk at the suggestion. The two whiled away the hours in deep conversation. In broken English, Rocancourt told Gry assorted tales from his past, at one point confessing to robbing a bank and "doing bad things." But he wanted to change; he wanted to live a good life. And he needed Gry to walk by his side, as he reinvented himself for real, this time.

Rocancourt was creating a fairytale in which Gry was the beautiful maiden and Rocancourt the knight in shining armour who, like a phoenix, would rise from the ashes of self-destruction and become a better man. Gry believed in Rocancourt's gentle manner and began spending more and more time with him. One day in October 1992, while the two were in Las Vegas, they got married. Just like that. Less than six months after they first met. Soon, a baby was on the way.

But Gry had doubts. Although she cared for the man who had managed to sneak a wedding ring onto her finger, and despite the fact he'd shared so much of his past with her, Gry didn't know a lot about her husband. Creditors called constantly, though family never did, and Rocancourt's story about a diplomat father didn't make any sense. She wasn't even sure how Rocancourt made a living. Once in a while, he'd share another deep dark secret with her, and Gry began to wonder what else he was hiding. What if he was a drug dealer?

Not long after they married, Gry demanded that Rocancourt tell her everything. Rocancourt complied, telling her that he was a member of the Italian mafia and a hardened criminal. No association to the mafia was ever proven, but it was quite possible Rocancourt had told so many stories that he couldn't differentiate truth from fable. What was less doubtful, and becoming increasingly clear, was that Rocancourt was a criminal.

Gry's response was to move in with her sister. For months, Rocancourt continued to call his estranged wife who, by now, was ready to give birth. Rocancourt promised that, once their baby was born, he'd be the kind of father that he never had, and he begged and pleaded to reunite with Gry. She stood firm, told him it was over and was actually frightened, a little, by his bizarre behaviour. Overwhelmed by Rocancourt's unwanted attention and running out of ideas on how to deal with him, Gry called the FBI's San Francisco office. Gry told *Vanity Fair* reporters that she wasn't sure why she made the call, nor what she expected to gain from it; she'd done it on a whim. But five minutes later, the FBI was at her door.

If Gry had doubts about her suspicions, that perhaps hormonal changes that come with pregnancy were causing her to blow everything out of proportion, those doubts were quickly put to rest by FBI agent Mark Irish. Unbeknownst to Rocancourt, the FBI had been watching him for some time. Irish told Gry that the FBI had initially begun their investigation on behalf of Swiss authorities but had subsequently found "a string of people in Sausalito and the Napa Valley who claimed Rocancourt had swindled them." Rocancourt had eluded the FBI, but, at one point, they tracked him to San Francisco's Fairmont Hotel, and, though Rocancourt had disappeared, an employee handed investigators Rocancourt's duffel bag. Inside, along with his clothes, was a 22-calibre pistol. The employee told FBI agents that Rocancourt had threatened him, that he had an "Uzi machine gun and two hand grenades" in his possession and that, if he crossed Rocancourt, he'd find himself dead.

By now, Gry was even more frightened, but she agreed to help the FBI find Rocancourt, on several occasions talking to him on the phone in an effort to help the FBI discover his location. Rocancourt must have had some way of preventing investigators from closing in on him, possibly by blocking his phone signal, because they weren't able to find him for some time. And then, one day in June 1993, investigators asked Gry to have Rocancourt call her the next morning, to tell him that she'd had enough and needed to break free from their relationship. She never understood why the FBI asked her to do this, nor how they decoded the scrambled phone signal they must have been receiving previously, but, within minutes of Gry saying her final goodbyes, Rocancourt called back. He'd been arrested in Las Vegas. He knew she was the catalyst by which investigators finally found him. "Nobody could have done this to me but you," Gry recalled Rocancourt saying, in her interview with *Vanity Fair*. He had added, "You don't have to worry about your life, because I'll never kill you." Gry now knew her husband was far more capable of violence than she'd ever imagined, so Rocancourt's last words to her before being taken away by the FBI gave her a small measure of relief.

Both Gry and the FBI thought the Christophe Rocancourt saga was over—that, after his extradition to Switzerland, he'd be locked up in a Geneva jail for a long time to come. They were wrong. Because the Swiss didn't have enough evidence to incarcerate Rocancourt, he was turned over to the French police to face numerous charges in that country. It was good news for the con man—his exploits in France were far less serious than those he was suspected of committing in Geneva. And, although he found himself behind bars in a prison just outside Paris in 1994, the incarceration was short-lived.

It was Rocancourt's letters to his daughter that touched Gry's heart. Despite having had enough of the strained relationship that left her forever changed, she had to admit Rocancourt's missives renewing his promise to be a good father were sweet and gentle. Almost daily, Rocancourt's correspondence made its way into Gry's mailbox, and his pen was obviously as eloquent as his spoken words because, by the time he was released in the summer of 1995, Gry had agreed to join him in France. Their reunion, during which time Rocancourt followed Gry back to Los Angeles, was brief. Gry's better judgment eventually won out, and, even when a Christian friend told her that Rocancourt had changed, was renewed in the Spirit and committed to a relationship with God, Gry didn't bite. She knew that if she wanted her daughter to have any kind of a normal life, she had to break free from the paralyzing hold Rocancourt had on her. She was done.

She also decided that, for the time being, she'd keep the fact that she'd had the marriage annulled while Rocancourt was in jail to herself.

MOVING ON—SORT OF

It's not clear when Rocancourt realized that he and Gry were really history, but he didn't remain distraught for long. His singleness was short-lived, and he was soon dating Playboy Playmate Pia Reyes. The two married in 1996, but Rocancourt still hadn't forgotten Gry. Shortly after Pia bore a son the couple named Zeus, Rocancourt was again begging for Gry's attention. Model and actress Rhonda Rydell was also on the periphery. Although Rydell didn't initially know her new love was married and still wooing his ex-wife at the same time, when she did find out, the news didn't seem to alter her affection for the con man. "He just has a very powerful spirit," Rydell told *People* magazine in 2000. "His lifestyle is crazy, but he also really believes in family. He has tremendous values."

Along with Gry and Reyes, Rocancourt tested those "values" on other members of the fairer sex, allegedly baiting a number of wealthy women with his charming ways and false promises, while being married to Reyes and, at times, maintaining his relationship with Rydell. His suave demeanour garnered him no end of affluent women looking for a little love and excitement, and, once he had them hanging on his every word, he'd take his usual next step: he'd make them an offer they couldn't refuse. There was always an investment opportunity of some kind or another that he swore would provide double or triple returns in just a few weeks. He was such a nice guy that few questioned his motives. Once these often-vulnerable women were on board, Rocancourt offered to purchase those investments on their behalf, acting as a middleman of sorts. "No, no trouble at all," he'd tell them. Of course, as soon as he had their money, he'd disappear, with his wallet considerably thicker and the women he was "helping" a lot less flush—or that's the way his alleged victims tell it.

Sometimes, he'd romance a woman, endear himself to her, get welcomed into her home and her life. He'd make her believe she was beautiful, that she was the cougar who'd hooked a younger man. Then, when she wasn't looking, he'd disappear, sometimes along with her valuables.

At the same time, Rocancourt had made friends with two new acquaintances, both State Department employees, and together the three were busy printing false passports. After chasing

Rocancourt for years, Los Angeles district attorney George Mueller finally had something concrete to pin on Rocancourt, a crime that he could prove his suspect was involved in, and, on December 5, 1997, the slippery cheat was arrested. Finally, the cops had their man, and he wouldn't be going anywhere for quite some time. Mueller might have been a little concerned when, in March 1998, Rocancourt posted the $100,000 bail and was released until his trial, but Mueller knew he had a strong case and was confident that Rocancourt's freedom would be short-lived. Apparently everyone involved underestimated Rocancourt's ability to come up with the bail money, as well as his potential as a flight risk, because as soon as the bond was paid, Rocancourt disappeared.

What Rocancourt was up to during the almost two years between his 1998 release on bail and his arrival in Manhattan in the winter of 1999 isn't clear. It appears he was lying low, managing to stay out of trouble, and spent several months vacationing with a buddy named Charles Glenn in such Asian hotspots as Jakarta, Bangkok and Hong Kong. Rocancourt always knew how to party and to surround himself with rich and beautiful people—people who, after they got to know him, didn't balk at paying Rocancourt's way, on occasion. It was almost as if the people he met needed to demonstrate in a concrete way their appreciation for Rocancourt's company. As one friend said to *New York Times* reporters Alan Feuer and Charlie LeDuff, "You could drop him into Nigeria, and in three weeks he would own the place."

Yes, he was having a great time, successfully mixing with the best of company and living the best of lifestyles. But the fun began to wear thin. Rocancourt missed the frenzied rush of life with America's rich; he probably even missed the run and chase between himself, his victims and law enforcement. Things moved more quickly in the Western world, a plus for adrenalin junkies like Rocancourt, and he decided to announce his return by giving district attorney Mueller, his old nemesis, a call. Mueller told *Dateline NBC* that Rocancourt suggested the two meet for tea and get to know each other: "you would really like me. We could become friends," he told Mueller. "And if you do arrest me I'll just bail out and flee the country anyway." Rocancourt's arrogance was annoying, especially to those who knew he was up to no good, but even if more than enough evidence to put him away for a long time came to light, the last time Rocancourt was in custody proved he couldn't be nailed down long enough to lock the doors behind him and toss away the key.

NEW YORK, NEW YORK

Shortly after his telephone call to Mueller, Rocancourt made his debut in the Big Apple. His incarnation, this time, was a Rockefeller—"but just call me Christopher." As a Rockefeller visiting New York's Upper East Side, he passed himself off as a wealthy financier, interested in investment options in the entertainment industry. He also started flirting with rich women again. According to *Vanity Fair,* one woman who didn't want to be identified said she gave Rocancourt $90,000 in cash, and when he suddenly left her, she noticed that more than $250,000 worth of watches and jewellery were missing from her home. Although that kind of loss would leave most of the real world destitute, for this woman, it was more embarrassing to lodge a formal complaint than the monetary loss was worth.

Rockefeller counted on that—it was exactly this kind of pride and avarice, he told reporters, it was his mission to challenge. It was also how he got away with so many of his alleged schemes. After all, no one, especially a wealthy individual with a large portfolio and a powerful position in society, wants to be thought of as gullible—most people who'd taken Rocancourt up on his investment "opportunities" were too embarrassed to admit they'd been duped by him. And yet, somehow, there was no end of possible victims for Rocancourt's schemes. Even when notable individuals were pointing his way and telling their friends to steer clear, people were conned. Even Tom Gregory, a New York stockbroker who met Rocancourt in the Hamptons, was conned by Rocancourt, giving him a $50,000 down payment for a $500,000 loan Rocancourt promised him. This was another alleged scam that Rocancourt sometimes pulled off. The loans, of course, never came through; the down payments made it only as far as Rocancourt's wallet and, like Gregory's $50,000, were never seen again.

Rocancourt skipped out on hotel and apartment bills while spending extravagant amounts of money at flashy night-clubs, downing Dom Perignon or Moet & Chandon and flirting with the rich and powerful. The money he flashed reinforced his image as a man of means. But cheques kept bouncing, promised investments never panned out and other people's money continued to disappear. Still, Rocancourt's demeanour never betrayed his true personality, never gave away his underhanded schemes. It never crossed anyone's mind that the bills Rocancourt tossed on the table to pay his tab were probably from the pocket of an admiring friend. He never flinched, not unless it was part of his ruse, and, as far as he was concerned, anyone he conned deserved what he or she got. "I feel sorry for their greed. I am not laughing. There is nothing funny about stupidity," he told the *New York Times* during a telephone interview he granted reporters in November 2000, while on the lam and living in what he referred to as an "English-speaking country."

Later, in an autobiography penned while sitting in a Canadian jail, Rocancourt said he considered himself a physician of sorts, whose job it was to "cure the rich of greed." Apparently, he felt no cognitive dissonance over the comment and blindly accepted his own greed in the process. "I became the reflection of their own vanities," he said.

It was in New York that Rocancourt met Gines Serran-Pagan. Pagan was an enigma himself. He was also one of the few who didn't fall for Rocancourt's charade and generally agreed with what was, in time, reported as the con artist's assessment of himself. Pagan was also one of Rocancourt's few acquaintances who didn't feel sorry for his victims. "He does not belong in jail," Pagan told *Vanity Fair*. "The people who gave him money, they belong in jail. For stupidity."

Pagan would later admit he wasn't aware of the extent of Rocancourt's deceit, nor of the number of victims he left behind, when he made that comment. It wasn't general knowledge then that Rocancourt had been fingered as a possible suspect in a shooting along Santa Monica Boulevard and was wanted for questioning in at least one suspicious death during his escapades in Los Angeles—Rocancourt denies these allegations to this day. But people were starting to get seriously suspicious about this supposed "Rockefeller." And the law was closing in.

So, as it turned out, was Pagan.

Saturday, July 29, 2000

Rocancourt had been getting to know Pagan, a Spanish-born painter who'd set up a studio in a 300-year-old red barn located not too far from Southampton's downtown core. Rocancourt had his eye on several of the artist's works, in particular, a piece called *Sunset in Quilin*. He told Pagan that he planned to buy the painting, along with one or two others; he even offered to have his bank wire Pagan the money, all $500,000 worth, directly into Pagan's overseas bank account.

He just needed the painter's bank account number. It was a proposition Pagan had to think about.

In the meantime, the painter had decided to host a summer soiree. It was an admittedly modest affair by Hamptons standards, the menu featuring soup, salad and a one-dish pasta. But the company was anything but modest, at least, as far as Rocancourt was concerned. Rocancourt, acting as a Rockefeller, was perhaps the biggest name at the table, but Pagan had informed him that other notable guests would also be in attendance. According to Pagan, the dinner guests included two heiresses of an unnamed Greek shipping mogul, the daughter of a top executive from Sony International's Tokyo offices and an art collector. This was Rocancourt's kind of crowd.

The dinner party was scheduled for 7:00 PM—it was a beautiful night for an al fresco meal, and the guests had gathered in Pagan's living room, waiting to proceed to dinner, long before Rocancourt, accompanied by his lady of the moment, a buxom blonde named Laurent, and Joseph, his balding, cell phone–bearing assistant, arrived at 9:00 PM. Pagan had started to worry. He'd gone to great lengths to play out his little game.

Pagan was convinced the man who called himself a Rockefeller was a phony, and so he'd planned to catch him at his own game, arranging the dinner as a ruse. Pagan's guests were actually Maria Eftimiades, *People* magazine's New York bureau chief, and her friend Clea, a lawyer with the U.S. Navy, masquerading as the two shipping heiresses. The art collector was Peter Fazio, a contractor and a friend of Pagan and his family, and the Sony executive's daughter was a photojournalist named Natsuko Utsumi. Pagan had planned the evening to see if he and his friends could find out a little more about the mysterious "Rockefeller" who had invaded the Hamptons. Maybe they could even catch him at his own game. "I just wanted us to join the movie that he was living," Pagan told *People* in 2000.

Rocancourt would later rebuke Pagan in the media, saying that he was quite aware of being played that night, but both parties had allowed the mock dinner party to continue unhindered. When Rocancourt finally arrived, he was greeted with the usual polite smiles, nods of acknowledgement, handshakes and bows of respect that he'd begun to expect when he entered a room; people were so polite in the Hamptons. Playing a Rockefeller gave Rocancourt a lot of respect—it was an old name with old money to back it.

"Christopher Rockefeller," Pagan said, introducing his tardy guest.

"Just call me Christopher," Rockefeller said, smiling. He always said that when he was introduced to someone.

Pagan suggested Rockefeller spend a little time with the shipping heiresses to pick their brains about what to consider when choosing a $34-million yacht—Rocancourt had once told Pagan he was planning to buy one. Rockefeller surely flashed them one of his endearing smiles, perhaps even took their hands in his and, leaning in just a little and never losing eye contact until the last possible moment, planted a kiss on each cheek.

Shortly after the initial pleasantries, the group moved outside. It was a beautiful evening, accompanied by polite dinner conversation. At one point, Pagan excused himself, went into the house and returned with a jug of red wine. Rockefeller praised the wine's rich bouquet and asked if it was a Bordeaux.

"No, no," Pagan said, looking embarrassed to have run out of the fine wines he usually served guests and explaining that he'd had to resort to opening a cheaper wine normally reserved for punch.

Rockefeller didn't seem to notice his faux pas. He went on talking about Hong Kong's best hotels, quoting Nietzsche, Kierkegaard and Kant and reiterating his promise to buy Pagan's *Sunset in Quilin*.

"Your account number, Pagan. Just give me your account number, and the money will go directly into your account."

This time, Pagan didn't hide his smile.

Meanwhile, pretending to be intrigued with the self-proclaimed heir to the Rockefeller fortune, one of the Greek shipping heiresses snapped Rockefeller's picture just as he was raising a soup spoon to his mouth. Rockefeller didn't blink, but the flash caught the attention of his aide.

"No, no pictures," the man yelled, startled by the gall the woman displayed, taking a picture without first asking permission. You don't treat a Rockefeller that way!

Joseph demanded the film from the woman; he would pay well for it, he said, flashing her a wad of bills. The young woman didn't want to sell her "vacation" photographs; they were far more important to the shipping heiress than whatever cash Joseph could offer. A verbal tug-of-war ensued. It was Rocancourt who finally calmed the situation.

"It's like Pagan says," he told his aide. "The lady, she just wants a souvenir, and what better souvenir than a photo of a Rockefeller? Leave her be. It's okay. She's okay."

It was past midnight when the guests finally left Pagan's home. Rocancourt and his entourage piled into his gold Mazda 626, an unassuming choice of vehicle for a Rockefeller, to be sure, but "Christopher" made a habit of turning up at the best restaurants wearing a pair of jeans and a baseball cap, so perhaps he chose to appear understated.

Turning to bid his host farewell, Rockefeller made one last promise to wire Pagan the money for his paintings as soon as the painter gave him his account number. Pagan smiled. He'd called Rockefeller a genius that evening, defining the term as "a person who has control, who has no fear," and he meant it. But it was a compliment loaded with ammunition—Pagan, looking square into Rockefeller's eyes, let his guest know that, though the rest of the world might be fooled by his wiles, Pagan was on to him. Pagan knew Rockefeller wasn't who he said he was, he just wasn't sure what kind of game he was playing.

Rocancourt would later learn the depths of Pagan's suspicions. Although the artist liked the masquerading con man, he didn't trust him. Not even just a little. That's why Pagan never did provide Rocancourt with his bank account number.

In November 2000, just a few months after the dinner party, Rocancourt rebutted Pagan's criticisms in the media, saying he was well aware of the farcical event. "Please," he snubbed. "A one-dish pasta...in the Hamptons?"

One could argue that a one-dish pasta on a Hamptons dinner menu was just as believable as a Rockefeller with a thick, French accent. And what was up with that car? Every good con man knows an expensive set of wheels is as important as knowing the right people—or having good taste in wine. A Rockefeller would never confuse cheap wine with a Bordeaux, unless, of course, he was trying to avoid embarrassing his host. Yes, a Rockefeller would definitely be gracious in just such a circumstance.

Pagan might have had his suspicions, but the party hadn't provided him with any concrete proof to back them. When Rockefeller telephoned and once again asked Pagan for his bank account number, the painter firmly declined.

"Sorry, my friend. Me, I prefer cash. That is no problem, I trust?"

"No. No problem at all," Rockefeller replied. *Sunset in Quilin* was rapidly losing its appeal.

That Rockefeller never produced the money Pagan asked for the paintings wasn't a surprise for the artist. "He's a fake, but I liked the guy...I like the unusual," Pagan told Bryan Burrough of *Vanity Fair* in January 2001.

Pagan would soon learn that Rockefeller was a bigger "fake" than he could have imagined.

REALITY HITS...FOR A WHILE

Rocancourt soon discovered he was overstaying his welcome in the Hamptons. Although he was flashing $2000 at hot night clubs, fewer and fewer people were buying his Rockefeller claim.

Fifty-two-year-old Kevin McCrary didn't trust Rocancourt from the moment he laid eyes on him. McCrary's friend, a masseuse named Corine Eeltink, had already invested $14,000 with Rocancourt but was called away to a family emergency before she could give him the remaining $125,000 she owed. Eeltink asked McCrary to meet with Rocancourt and give him the money, but when McCrary met Rockefeller, he held back. Something about the man struck McCrary the wrong way.

McCrary's family knew the Rockefellers, and Rocancourt didn't resemble the Rockefellers McCrary knew in any way. Rocancourt could talk a lot but didn't always say much.

He could name-drop, claim associations with everyone from the late Dodi Al Fayed to former president Bill Clinton, but he seemed crude by Rockefeller standards, spoke with a strong French accent and kept questionable company. And his clothes—no Rockefeller would dress like that. The whole picture just didn't add up for McCrary.

After a couple of meetings, McCrary refused to give Rocancourt Eeltink's money and demanded that Rocancourt return her initial $14,000 investment. Angry phone calls between the two escalated until McCrary contacted the police. Unfortunately, McCrary had no concrete proof that Rocancourt was anything but an annoying fellow he'd had a falling out with. He had only suspicions. McCrary could pin no known crime on Rocancourt, until Rocancourt ditched on an $8000 bill for his lodgings at the Mill Garth, an East Hampton inn. "Bingo," McCrary thought.

On August 2, 2000, East Hampton detective Margaret Dunn arrested Rocancourt. By then, police had discovered a few more unpaid bills, and Rocancourt was charged with "theft of service" amounting to $19,000. He was also charged with false personation, which, according to *West's Encyclopedia of American Law* is defined as "falsely assuming the identity of another to gain a benefit or avoid an expense." Once again, Rocancourt was behind bars. He immediately hired defence attorney Bruce Cutler, the same lawyer the late mobster John Gotti used, and posted the $45,000 bail. Rocancourt was getting used to posting bail. "He didn't seem nervous when I met him there," Cutler told *People* magazine in 2000. "I didn't get the impression he was going to run."

Rocancourt even fooled Gotti's lawyer.

NEVER LET THEM SEE YOU SWEAT

Although any other person in Rocancourt's position might be at least a little nervous and willing to admit his game was up, Rocancourt didn't flinch at his New York arrest. It didn't seem to bother him that he skipped out on $45,000 bail, paid by a friend who obviously still believed in him, and that the police were now, more than ever, determined to hunt him down. Perhaps he thrived on the attention. He certainly knew what to do, and he began by getting a new dye job and passport and hopping a plane leaving the U.S. via California.

At this point in the investigation, Rocancourt remained one-up on his would-be captors. Police still weren't sure who the man calling himself Christopher Rockefeller really was. At his arrest in the Hamptons, police uncovered a passport in his possession under the name of Fabien Ortuno, which they reasoned could be his real name, but, as the investigation developed, it became clear that Rocancourt had as many aliases as he had stories. He alternately went by the given names Christopher, Christoph, Christophe, Chris, Fabien, James, Michael, Prince Galitzine Christo and Thierre Daniel.

He had an equally impressive list of assumed surnames: Rocancourt, Lononcour, Lononcourt, Lenancour, Lenancourt, Ortuno, Rockefeller, Gauvin, De Laurentiis, Reyes, Lloyd, Fox and Van Hoven.

Police also eventually pieced together the charges brought against Rocancourt under those names: sexual assault and assault with a deadly weapon, criminal possession of a weapon, false personation and passport forgery, robbery and theft of services, grand larceny and attempted grand larceny, fraud, criminal possession of a forged instrument (which simply means possessing any document containing forged information) and offering a false instrument for filing.

Although authorities were working hard to find out what they could of Rocancourt's true identity, by the fall of 2000, they were no closer to learning his whereabouts. During Rocancourt's November 2000 interview with reporters from the *New York Times,* he committed only to saying that his location was an English-speaking country. The interview wasn't geared to unveiling Rocancourt's exploits; it focused on unveiling the real Christophe Rocancourt, on getting to know the man who'd become somewhat of a mystery worldwide. Rocancourt wanted to explain, in his own words, who he really was and to refute some of the accusations being made against him—to "redefine the contours and colors [sic] of his personality." He didn't seem to appreciate the portrait that the media had painted of him.

"I would not consider myself a criminal—I steal with my mind," Rocancourt told the *New York Times,* though he did cop to stealing and lying. "If I take things, if that is your definition of a criminal, then I am a criminal."

Rocancourt also denied allegations of his involvement in a shoot-out in West Hollywood that ended with one dead, saying that killing was the "ultimate sin" and he'd never do such a thing; he was a good Catholic. "I don't believe in taking another life. It is the ultimate sin." When reporters asked Rocancourt if thought he'd ever get caught, he simply answered, "That is in the hands of God…If they catch me, I will make no deal. I will do my time."

And catch him they did, because "the Mounties always get their man."

The Canadian Connection, Part II

Rocancourt was captured in Oak Bay without incident.

"He was co-operative during the arrest, but we did exercise caution given his history and utilized the services of the (emergency) response team," Detective Sergeant Ron Coulls of the Oak Bay police told Dene Moore of the Canadian Press. Officers took both Rocancourt and Pia into custody, and officials from the BC Children's Ministry took temporary custody of the teary and frantic four-year-old Zeus.

Rocancourt must have been surprised to find himself in handcuffs and on his way to jail here, in Canada, where he'd made few enemies and hadn't once hit the papers. Who could have tipped off investigators of his whereabouts, and what exactly did Canadian officials have on him?

Rocancourt was about to learn that, although Canadians might be considered polite and mild mannered, they certainly aren't pushovers. Rocancourt's arrest came down to a single, official complaint lodged against him by a Vancouver couple, businessman Robert Baldock and his wife, Norma. The pair had fallen victim to one of Rocancourt's scams, losing what might be considered petty cash in the Hamptons but was almost everything the Baldocks had. Once Rocancourt and his wife were in custody, it was only a matter of time before police plugged a fingerprint into the system and pulled up an FBI "wanted" status for the con man.

The first order of business was to confirm that the man in custody in Victoria was indeed Christophe Rocancourt. As the book on the new guy in town opened wider and wider, it was quickly apparent that the man sitting in a Canadian jail cell was none other than the "fake Rockefeller" of the Hamptons highlife and that he was a lot more dangerous than he at first appeared. The police learned about Rocancourt's arrest warrants in the U.S., France and Switzerland—later discovering that Rocancourt had faced the charges in France and Switzerland before coming to Canada. As a steady stream of information flowed into police headquarters, an eager media soaked up everything they could, keeping Rocancourt's story in the public spotlight and working with their U.S. colleagues to get all the juicy details.

Investigators discovered that, while in Canada, Rocancourt was posing as an international Formula One racecar driver and, for the most part, was living under his real name. But he was still trying to con anyone he could out of money, and when he met the Baldocks through a mutual acquaintance, he introduced himself as Michael Van Hoven. Some reports alleged Rocancourt defrauded the Vancouver businessman of more than $150,000.

On his arrest, Rocancourt was also charged with sexual assault, assault causing bodily harm and uttering a threat to cause death or bodily harm stemming from an alleged altercation with a 24-year-old woman from Victoria, BC. In a preliminary hearing, Rocancourt was ordered to stand trial on these charges, and a court date was set for the spring of 2002. Information related to the assault was under a publication ban, but Rocancourt ultimately didn't spend much time inside a courtroom on that case, because charges were inexplicably dropped in January 2002.

Charges laid against Pia at the time of her arrest were eventually stayed. She pleaded ignorant of Rocancourt's alleged misdeeds. "I thought he was doing business. He keeps me out of his business," she told reporters, visibly happy to be released yet dazed from the experience.

Rocancourt wasn't so lucky. Despite his dimpled grin and dreamy eyes, his demeanour didn't sway the Canadian courts. Crown prosecutor Miriam Maisonville spared no details in telling the court that, while Rocancourt and his family were enjoying Whistler's finest, often on someone else's coin, Rocancourt had become acquainted with Baldock. He claimed to be a millionaire and gained Baldock's confidence. Baldock told Rocancourt about an interesting new business venture he was involved in called Heartlink Canada Inc. The company was trying to develop a unique heart monitor that compiled information on an individual's heart rate. The theory behind the work was the belief that there might be a correlation between an individual's heart rate and mental illness. It was a noble quest, and Baldock heartily believed in his proposal to create the device needed to collect this information. He was close, so very close, to moving from the drawing board to the assembly line, but the company needed more money.

When Baldock met Rocancourt, he must have thought his worries were over, especially when Rocancourt offered to invest $5 million in Baldock's business. Thrilled with the possibility of having such a generous benefactor, Baldock kept the champagne flowing.

According to the *Vancouver Sun,* Rocancourt continued building his image by telling Baldock that he drove his racecar for Ferrari, "that he had more than $250 million in assets, and that his European father was very rich." He also told Baldock of a $28-million contract he said he had with Ferrari—that's the kind of money a top racecar driver could command for a company sponsorship, he said.

On one occasion, to cement the rich-boy image Rocancourt was trying to uphold, Rocancourt wrote a $100,000 cheque while in Baldock's presence—a deposit on a Whistler chalet, he explained. In the meantime, Baldock was paying for Rocancourt's apartment on West Hastings, along with his travel expenses, car rentals and incidentals. Although this isn't completely out of the ordinary for a legitimate business deal of this magnitude, Baldock eventually left the relationship without a penny to put toward his business venture and a raft of bills left behind by Rocancourt and his family.

The evidence against Rocancourt was overwhelming. Faced with the realization that he'd never get out of going to trial on charges of defrauding the Baldocks, Rocancourt played the hand that made the most sense and might even win him a few brownie points for saving the court's time and money—he pleaded guilty. Judge Conni Bagnall called Rocancourt's fraud against the Baldocks a "financial predatory scheme" and said that "the fraud was possible because [Rocancourt was] a talented and brazen liar."

Despite sharing a relationship with more ups and downs than a rollercoaster ride, Pia never wavered in her support for the father of her son, at least, not publicly. "I believe he's an innovative, creative, imaginative person," Pia told Canadian

Press reporters. "To me, he's very exciting. It's like I'm married to a hundred different men."

An average sentence for the crime Rocancourt confessed to, even with leniency given for a guilty plea, carries with it a jail term of two or three years. Shockingly, on Friday, June 14, 2002, Judge Bagnall sentenced Rocancourt to a single day, plus timed served. The reason for the laughable sentence was that Rocancourt had already been in custody for 14 months since his arrest, and time served before sentencing is worth double its value. Rocancourt had been handed a get-out-of-jail-free card—except for the demand that he repay the money he owed the Bagnalls. Although they would probably never see all the money they lost, the $16,000 cash in Rocancourt's possession when he was arrested was supposed to go directly to his victims, along with a Rolex watch and a laptop.

Pia was ecstatic about the sentence. Rocancourt grinned and, according to an article in the *Vancouver Sun,* even waved to the courtroom sketch artist. Rocancourt's lawyer, Mayland McKimm, said his client was ready to go straight. No more con games for him. He was eager to turn over a new leaf. In fact, Rocancourt hadn't wasted his time in jail, waiting for his trial. No undirected energies for him, no, no, no. He used the time to write the French version of his autobiography, *I, Christophe Rocancourt, Orphan, Playboy and Convict,* and, although it's against the law for criminals to profit from stories of their criminal activities, in the years to come, Rocancourt would say that he could make as much money on the book and its subsequent movie rights as he did being a con artist—around $40 million by his estimate. (Somehow Rocancourt was allowed to keep 25 percent of the proceeds from his story, with the remaining 75 percent to be divided among his victims.) To this point, Rocancourt hasn't proven to be a pillar of truth, so it behooves the skeptic in us all to think twice before taking him seriously...but you never know.

DON'T LOOK NOW

Whatever relief Rocancourt and his wife might have felt at having done his time for his Canadian crime was short-lived. Pia's plans for an electric, exciting future with her talented husband appeared to hit a few roadblocks. As soon as U.S. officials heard of Rocancourt's impending release, they were ready to present their case at an extradition hearing. Rocancourt was a popular man, wanted in two jurisdictions, in New York and in California. Knowing he'd be fighting a losing battle, Rocancourt waived his right to an extradition hearing in each case and surrendered. On April 13, 2003, newspaper headlines read, "Pretender may be heir to jail time"; "Counterfeit Rockefeller agrees to be extradited"; and "Conman faces U.S. court, counterfeit Rockefeller agrees to extradition charges." Officials south of the border were anxious to get their hands on the slippery con, lock a pair of cuffs on his wrists and not let him out of their sight.

There was no eluding investigators, this time, and Rocancourt knew he'd have to face the music. In May 2003, he pleaded guilty to federal fraud charges in exchange for a plea bargain when it came to jail time. As well, he'd face deportation the moment he was released from prison. Rocancourt would miss living in the U.S., but without the deal, he could face 20 years in a federal penitentiary, and even Rocancourt might have found that too tough to smile through. "I take responsibility for my actions...I apologize for what I did wrong," Rocancourt said during his sentencing hearing in October 2003. He was given three years and 10 months in federal prison for one set of charges and a concurrent sentence of up to five years for charges brought against him in Suffolk County, New York. In March 2004, the remaining charges against Rocancourt were heard, and the French con man received another five years in prison, also to be served concurrently with his original two sentences. Rocancourt's lawyer, Victor Sherman, told reporters that Rocancourt got "a great deal," in which all his cases were resolved in "basically one sentence."

What Rocancourt missed when it came to making an honest living he appeared to more than make up for in luck. In October 2006, the man Hamptonites and the rest of the world had come to know as the fake Rockefeller was chauffeured from Pennsylvania's Allenwood federal prison in a plain, unmarked van. He wasn't just a free man who had served his time. He was being deported, sent back to France—unconfirmed stories suggested that authorities even bought him a first-class plane ticket.

Shortly after his release, Rocancourt agreed to an interview with *Dateline*. Although he had pleaded guilty to the charges he'd just served time for, and had agreed he wasn't always honourable, he balked when it came to saying he was a con man. "I've been a 'confidence man'...I agree with that. But the 'con man....'" Rocancourt wouldn't own up to what he called the "corny" short form of the term.

When it came right down to it, Rocancourt saw himself as an actor who took on different personas or a doctor interested in healing the rich of their greedy ways and prescribing his own unique form of morality. Rocancourt told *Dateline* that he still couldn't believe that anyone would buy the Rockefeller gig. "How you for a minute can be serious to think when you don't have to know history to say, 'Hey, Rockefeller, your French accent? There's no Rockefeller in France.' C'mon, use your brain." It was greed, Rocancourt said, that blinded his victims to the truth, and maybe even a little vanity. All it took were fancy restaurants, the best champagne and being the first to pick up the tab to have people eating out of the palm of his hand. Rocancourt told *Dateline* that the largest tab he covered was in the neighbourhood of $80,000, and because that kind of cash could represent a third of the price of an average U.S. home, it was easy to believe he was loaded.

The way Rocancourt described it, his game wasn't diffi-cult. You just had to be a great actor with pretty solid self-esteem. But he was through with the con game, he said. There came a time in your life where looking over your shoulder and worry-ing about meeting up in a dark alley with someone whose life savings you took loses its appeal. "No, you can be a good player, but there is a time where you just retreat, you know? You have to stop it," Rocancourt said. "I think it's a closed chapter."

In reality, though, Rocancourt no longer needed to rely on the con game to maintain his place in the limelight. He'd managed to make himself as widely known as many movie stars. Now, he could rely on his success as an author and entertainer, for his notoriety and for his history as the man who'd kept authorities running for years. Not long after his autobiography was published in French, it was translated into English and retitled *The French Hustler*. His subsequent book, *Hoaxes*, was also a bestseller.

In addition to his writing success, Rocancourt was becoming an actor, escorting model Naomi Campbell at the 2009 Cannes Film Festival and making plans to appear in French filmmaker Catherine Breillat's movie, *Bad Love*—the story of an actress who has an affair with an impostor.

Rocancourt continued to make headlines following his appearance with Campbell. He was photographed rubbing elbows with French politicians at the Elysée Palace, French president Nicolas Sarkozy's official residence, during an awards ceremony for a filmmaker friend. Thomas Langmann, one of France's newest hot producers, was planning a movie on Rocancourt's life called *A.K.A.*—he got the idea, he says, from a segment of *Dateline* in which Rocancourt's life was described as being like a movie. As if that weren't enough, Rocancourt launched a clothing line shortly after returning to France and, in the fall of 2008, hosted for a series of French *National Geographic* TV documentaries.

Everyman's Dream?

For most of us, the vision of retiring comfortably in a cabin nestled on a remote lakeshore or snow-birding in Arizona for the winter is about as elaborate as our practical dreams allow. Summers in the Hamptons and winters on the Mediterranean are the stuff of movies and big dreamers with big bank accounts to support them. But Rocancourt didn't let his lowly birth and the poverty of his youth dictate his future. In his mind, he was everything he said he was—the Italian mobster, the executive movie producer and racecar driver, the vineyard owner and Sophia Loren's son or nephew. He basked in the limelight he produced for himself, enjoying the thrill of the chase, whether he was doing the chasing or was the one on the run. He served his time in prison, using it to his advantage, writing books and plotting his future. Maybe that's why, despite the financial carnage he left behind, an adoring public still drank him in. Yes, he'd walked crooked paths to get somewhere, but nothing stopped him from living his dream. In a warped kind of way, he represented the Everyman of today's society.

That so many people could inadvertently glorify crime through their support of Rocancourt was nothing short of disturbing, as far as Detective Mueller was concerned. He told *Dateline* that Rocancourt's rise to fame was the result of a pathetic fascination by a public that glorifies criminals. Mueller stressed that many people were hurt by Rocancourt's scams, and he had no doubt that Rocancourt would be back to his old ways at some point in the future. "Christopher is out for one person, and that's himself," Mueller said. "He's always been a liar. He's always been a cheater."

Rocancourt stayed out of trouble for quite some time following his release from prison. But if you looked a little closer, slipped him under a moral microscope, you could see the cracks, some of them pretty large, in the image built for himself. Rocancourt's personal life hadn't stabilized since his self-professed emancipation. He divorced Pia, and a relationship with former Miss France, Sonja Roland, lasted long enough to produce a daughter. But despite saying that his biggest regret was not being the father he wanted to be, Rocancourt eventually walked out of his relationship with Roland, too. It was like a disease; Rocancourt didn't seem to be able to stay put for very long. Investigators like Mueller were betting on the old adage that a leopard can't change its spots, and this appeared to be true for Rocancourt's personal life. Mueller was betting that it would also hold true for Rocancourt's criminal activities.

More than two years after Rocancourt's release, the ex-con seemed to be doing everything he could to prove Mueller wrong, at least, when it came to legal misconduct. Even the more jaded members of the public might have begun to believe that Rocancourt had changed. And then, in July 2009, Rocancourt found himself back in the spotlight, and not in a good way. The story had Rocancourt facing off with Catherine Breillat, who accused Rocancourt of defrauding her of 650,000 Euros. Diagnosed with cerebral vascular disease in 2004, Breillat was struggling with health issues. If Breillat's accusations were true, the con man wasn't just up to his old tricks; he was stooping to an all-time low. Breillat accused Rocancourt of "an abuse of weakness" and said she rued the day she met him—it was even worse, she said, than the day she received her diagnosis. Rocancourt might have written his version of his life story, but if Breillat had her way, the world would read about this latest chapter and learn of his exploits from a victim—she was planning to write a tell-all entitled *Rocancourt and Me*.

Was Mueller right? Was it possible that the king of modern-day con men, previously heralded by some for his personal efforts at rehabilitation, hadn't really changed his spots at all?

In August 2009, Rocancourt told the media that he was preparing to file a complaint for defamation. Because media reports on the standoff between Breillat and Rocancourt are scarce, the public will have to wait and see what the next chapter holds.

THE LAST WORD?

Despite his impoverished roots, Rocancourt could indeed be seen as a self-made man, of sorts. His story appeared in such prestigious newspapers as the *New York Times, The East Hampton Star* and the *New York Post*, the *Vancouver Sun* and *Vancouver Province*, the *Globe and Mail* and the *Guardian* in the U.K. Magazines such as *People* and *Vanity Fair* fought alongside *CNN, 60 Minutes, Dateline* and even *Court TV* to be the first to broadcast the most unusual rags-to-riches story ever, and online sources, such as the celebrity-focused Gala.fr, have also written about the man. Rocancourt has already published three books about his exploits, and, as of this writing, Maverick House—a publishing company whose mandate is to "publish socially and politically relevant non-fiction books" for the international market—plans to publish Rocancourt's latest rendition, *The Talented Mr. Rocancourt: The Memoirs of France's Most Notorious Conman*. How interesting that Rocancourt reneged on his earlier opposition to the "corny" word "con man." Ultimately, Rocancourt had become everything he'd hoped to be—he was famous, and, despite his criminal past, people still found him interesting. He might even argue that, yes, he felt loved.

But make no mistake; Rocancourt is a crook who, despite semantics, is nothing more than a con man. For all his bravado, all the gold and diamonds he flashed, the bad cheques he wrote, the promises he broke, Rocancourt is a poor orphan boy who, at any cost, was looking for an easy way to make it in the world.

Nothing more.

Chapter Five

It's Not My Fault

KLAUS BURLAKOW, A.K.A. PATRICK BURKE, TIMOTHY MICHAEL COLLINS

~

*I couldn't cope...There was a bizarre and rather
threatening set of circumstances...I had become involved
in a situation I felt I couldn't cope with, and in the end
I was quite terrified for myself and my family.*

–Klaus Burlakow, during his sentencing hearing on
seven counts of armed robbery

THE PERFECT HOST

Competing in the Olympics is the dream of every high-performance athlete. During the heat of training, they only need to close their eyes and they're in the stadium, feeling the electricity, gooseflesh all over, the applause from the crowd almost deafening, even if it is only imaginary. The Pan American Games are like a warm-up for Olympic-level athletes in the Americas. Held the year before each Olympics, the Pan Am Games allows contenders to get a feel for their colleagues in their respective fields and much-needed experience in a high-powered competition—an athlete needs to learn how to stay focused amid all the excitement.

In 1999, Winnipeg, Manitoba, was hosting the event, and organizers were anxiously planning for the arrival of the 5000 athletes expected to descend on the city and neighbouring towns. The Games ran from July 23 to August 8, and hundreds of workers and volunteers spent long hours during those two weeks monitoring venues, transporting athletes and making sure visitors to the Windy City left with fond memories of Canada's "friendly" province.

It took years of planning to prepare for every conceivable eventuality in what was one of the biggest events to come to Winnipeg at that time, and the man in the driver's seat, making sure that everything worked like a well-oiled machine, was Klaus Burlakow. The Winnipeg civil servant had a lot of experience in event planning and had worked with the City for almost three decades before Mayor Susan Thompson, the city's 40th incumbent in the big chair, appointed Burlakow as the city representative for the Games. In 1996, a news story reported that Thompson had spent $130 million worth of tax money in preparation for the event. With that kind of coin to spend, Burlakow not only had a dream job but also had a pretty decent budget to work with.

He also had the added excitement of preparing for the royal visit of Princess Ann. She was scheduled to arrive in Winnipeg on July 22 and planned to spend several days in the "Peg."

Although Burlakow wasn't responsible for looking after her during the entire visit, he was involved with her stop at City Hall. The red carpet was done away with—the good princess didn't want the city to shoulder any unnecessary expenses—but the customary velvet rope erected to keep an adoring public the required six metres back was still a go. Every aspect of her safety and comfort were dealt with, including an inspection of the mayor's private facilities—nothing but three-ply tissue would do, should the princess need a moment to herself.

After Burlakow's many years as a mid-level administrator, working in various city departments, his elevation to events coordinator for the Pan Am Games must have represented an exciting change of pace. Burlakow appeared to have enjoyed the challenge and followed up the success of the 1999 event with others—Winnipeg has a reputation for being one of this country's cultural hotspots. In 2001, Burlakow was again in the spotlight as organizer of another Winnipeg first, an event called Get Together Downtown. What was touted as the "biggest-ever block party" saw the city's busy Portage Avenue closed from Main Street to Memorial Boulevard, and from July 13 to 15, the half dozen blocks or so were filled with vendors and street entertainers, and residents and visitors alike were treated to a classic prairie summer, Winnipeg style.

Overall, Burlakow had a few feathers in his cap. He had a good life: a wife and two kids, a house in the suburbs and a job that paid well and offered no end of variety. Burlakow was living the Canadian dream—or at least that was the way it seemed to anyone who knew him.

That dream was about to slip through his fingers.

A Change in Fortunes

In August 2001, Burlakow took early retirement from the City of Winnipeg for reasons that were never made public and began looking at a number of employment options. He had a lot of experience and had worked in various white-collar jobs before being employed by the City of Winnipeg. He was also used to living fairly well. News reports estimated Burlakow's income with the City was about $123,000 a year—a huge wage in a province with an average single-person income of $22,193, according to Statistics Canada 2005 figures. And although he allegedly received $100,000 from the City to, as reported in the media, "leave amicably," his little nest egg wasn't going to last forever—especially after taking his wife on a month-long holiday, buying a new Ford Expedition and furnishing his home with new appliances. He was used to living well, and jobs that paid the salary he was used to were few and far between.

In his search for a lucrative job, Burlakow started regularly travelling to Washington state, where he became acquainted with a woman named Cathy Taylor. According to an early interview Taylor conducted with Canadian Press, the Seattle-area woman was first introduced to the man she knew as Patrick

Burke some time in the late spring or early summer of 2002. Exactly what sort of relationship Burlakow and Taylor had isn't clear. But a year or so after Burlakow's eventual incarceration, Taylor spoke more freely with reporters from *Elle Canada,* a national women's magazine, admitting that she'd met Burlakow on an Internet chat room—she was Sleepless 777.

Burlakow apparently had spun Taylor a tale of woe: he was going through a divorce. From their correspondence, he recognized Taylor as a soft-hearted woman, and he was right. She felt sorry for him. The more she chatted with the man she knew as Burke, the more intrigued Taylor became.

As Taylor explains it, Burlakow wove a tale that would melt the hardest of hearts. During their first face-to-face meeting, a couple of months into their online friendship, Burlakow allegedly told Taylor that he had been married once before his current wife, quite possibly to the love of his life, based on the tears that Taylor said flowed freely when he spoke about his beloved Kathleen. Burlakow told Taylor that Kathleen had died tragically when an IRA bomb exploded near their apartment—she was outside at the time and was caught in the explosion. Burlakow told Taylor that he was originally from Belfast and that he'd been born into a poor family, a plight made more devastating by the death of his mother when he was just nine years old and by the ongoing abuses he suffered at the hands of his alcoholic father.

But according to his elaborate tale, Burlakow didn't let the circumstances of his youth limit him in any way. He just picked himself up and carried along, he told Taylor. It was his determination that pulled him from a life on the streets, his own hard work that earned him a university scholarship. And there was mystery in his life, too; at one point, he said he served as a spy with the Irish Republican Army. He was the ultimate poor boy made good; to hear him tell it, he was the very definition of a Renaissance man.

"I was fascinated by his intelligence, his background and his humour," Taylor told *Elle*. "I was totally at ease with him." As far as Taylor was concerned, she'd stumbled across a lonely millionaire, who wasn't afraid to lavish her with gifts and expensive meals, at one point even opening up his bank book for her to see.

Burlakow soon made monthly trips to the Seattle area and visited Taylor regularly. The pair began researching and laying the groundwork for a joint events-marketing venture; as Burlakow later explained, the relationship was a business venture with a woman who had similar interests and a solid and marketable idea. Taylor went on to explain that she believed Burlakow owned a house in Seattle and generally spent two or three weeks each month there. He also led her to believe he'd be making his permanent residence in Seattle—his divorce was getting ugly, and he was desperate to get away from Winnipeg and start over. His description was a little more poetic when, in 2003, Burlakow spoke with Susan Bourette, a correspondent with the *Globe and Mail*. "Eventually, I decided to break away from this life of quiet desperation. To leave Winnipeg, the seventh level of Hell. To allow the magic in my soul to ride the wind and see where it landed." When Burlakow met Cathy Taylor, he was ready to do just about anything to "ride the wind." He was so enamoured with his new, albeit make-believe, reality, he even managed to sweep her up with his enthusiasm.

Meanwhile, Burlakow was obliged to return to Winnipeg from time to time, to prevent his wife, who had yet to hear of any divorce rumours, from growing concerned. It was during one of those visits that Burlakow's leap into the bizarre really took hold.

ONE WINNIPEG WINTER

It was Wednesday, November 6, 2002—a "hump day," according to many weekday nine-to-fivers. It was also "Take Our Kids to Work Day," a day set aside each year for about 13,000 of Manitoba's Grade 9 students to accompany a friend or family member to work and learn what a typical day was like for them. This year, the day added some variety for one mother, who spent her working hours as a bank teller and was looking forward to having her 14-year-old son shadow her. Once the mother and son arrived at the Scotiabank at 1220 Pembina Highway, mom probably went over all the basics, explaining what the lad could and could not do, where he should stand when she was serving customers at the teller's booth, the importance of client confidentiality, that kind of thing. The boy was probably excited, if for no other reason than that the activity spelled eight hours away from the classroom. He had no idea what a unique experience he'd have that day: it would be one he'd likely choose not to repeat, not for all the money in the world.

Those who work with the public meet all kinds of people, so when a man walked into the bank with a pack and headgear that was a little too warm for the weather, no one gave it much thought. Tellers were probably already speaking with a client or two. Or perhaps the bank staff was busy going through their regular checks and balances. But when the man with the pack sidled up to the woman's till, pulled out what looked like a gun and demanded cash, it wasn't just the teller whose heart started racing—what the 14-year-old boy standing beside his mother must have been thinking is hard to imagine. The woman later wrote a victim impact statement about the incident: "All I could think about was, 'Where's my son?' and, 'God, don't let this guy shoot me in front of him.'" But that day, all she could do was follow the man's instructions and empty her drawer, placing the money as quickly as possible into his bag.

Although the training is rarely put into practice, tellers faced with a robbery are instructed to follow bank protocol, which includes tucking a dye pack inside the money. A dye pack is typically attached to a small, bomb-like device equipped with a timer, but the practice isn't common knowledge. Unaware that the terrified teller had slipped the dye pack into the bag, the robber's plan for a quick payday was foiled shortly after he left the building, when the device exploded, showering the money around it with red ink. When the man reached into his backpack, the ink stained his hands, and, because he no doubt tried to salvage some of the cash, the staining would only have gotten worse. In the truest sense of the phrase, the guy was "caught red-handed." The bank robber hadn't gone far before realizing he'd been duped, and, frustrated by the entire experience, he dumped the bag in a back alley.

Klaus Burlakow had just committed his first robbery, and all he managed to accomplish was to terrorize a bank full of people and traumatize a mother and her young son.

Burlakow no longer worked for the City, but, in a very public way, he'd signalled the end of his glory days.

Although the spoils from Burlakow's bungled heist were soon discovered, no one had a clue about the robber's identity. The whole thing happened so quickly that Burlakow hadn't even made a clear impression on bank staff except, perhaps, on the teller who had stood with a gun pointed at her. She made a mental note of the way he moved, the way he spoke and his general appearance, and she tucked it all away in the back of her mind.

For now, however, Burlakow seemed to be safe. Except for the need to camouflage his hands, he'd weathered the experience fairly well. And the fact that police weren't at his door to arrest him likely lulled him into thinking that, if he got away with the crime once, he could probably get away with it again. He'd had a taste of the adrenalin that came with doing something he'd never imagined he could do. His staid, safe and very ordinary life had been infused with a bizarre kind of energy. Although he hadn't actually walked away with a bag full of cash, he had gained something else: experience. He'd be smarter next time. He had a better idea of what he would and wouldn't do, and the first decision he made was not to rush into anything.

With the Christmas holidays coming, he restrained himself, waiting until the New Year to strike again. He planned the next hold-up better, picking a target that was much farther from home yet not a place he would stay for any length of time. He'd be in and out of the community almost as fast as he'd be in and out of the bank.

ONE UNIQUE BUSINESS TRIP?

The friendship and business partnership between Taylor and Burlakow grew in equal increments, and in the relatively short time they'd been working together, the partners had already firmed up plans to host a large concert, with a big headliner, in April 2003. The two usually spent the weeks when Burlakow was in Seattle travelling throughout the Pacific Northwest, looking for business opportunities and meeting with potential clients. It was on just such a business trip, on Friday, January 10, 2003, that Taylor and Burlakow found themselves crossing the Washington state border, on their way to Vancouver, BC. They were travelling across the line for a business meeting, but for some reason, Burlakow didn't share the details with Taylor, insisting on going to the meeting alone. Although his behaviour might have seemed odd, Taylor reasoned that a man with the experience and clout of Burlakow certainly must have known what he was doing, and so she acquiesced. Had she been aware of Burlakow's plans, Taylor might have objected, but when later questioned about it, she pleaded ignorant of what came next.

Vancouver's winter weather is typically mild, and although the city does get snow on occasion, the month of January is more likely to be wet. Not having to trudge through snow was a plus for Burlakow—and rain washed away things, like footprints. Moments after walking into a branch of Scotiabank, at about 10:00 AM, Burlakow pulled out what witnesses said looked like a gun and asked for money. This time, he was smarter than he had been few months ago. This time, he'd planned better, taking every variable he could think of into account. He knew about messy dye packs, and when he demanded money from the tellers, he warned them, "No dye packs." This time, he made off with $2850 that he could actually use.

Although Burlakow's heart must have been racing when he left the bank, he managed to calm himself down enough to appear normal when he rejoined Taylor. His partner didn't suspect a thing, and the two left Vancouver, returning stateside as if nothing untoward had happened. Taylor said she never knew that her partner had thrust a gun at two bank tellers that day, until months later, when she heard the news that the man she knew as Patrick Burke, the man with the Irish accent and tales of survival from the war in Northern Ireland, who'd spent time with her and her friends and family, with whom she'd invested money, was allegedly involved in the robbery of nine banks. And that the day trip to Vancouver appeared to have been specifically tailored to hold up the Scotiabank there.

According to Taylor, she first learned of Burlakow's escapades a couple of months after the couple's trip to Vancouver, when Burlakow didn't show up for a morning meeting. It wasn't like him to blow her off like that and not even phone. When she tried calling him, she discovered that his cell phone number had been disconnected. As a last resort, without any other means of getting in touch with her partner and concerned that Burlakow might have been in an accident, Taylor went online to check out the Winnipeg news—and stumbled across some shocking stories of a city bureaucrat who'd been arrested and charged with robbing a bank. The mug shot glaring back at her from the computer screen looked like the man Taylor had invested so much time and money with, but it was the stories about Burlakow that curdled her blood.

"I almost fainted," she told the *Winnipeg Sun*. She'd never considered herself a pushover and didn't believe every story she'd heard or read in the media, for that matter. In fact, Taylor had proof her partner was who he said he was. She'd seen Burlakow's Manitoba driver's licence and his Canadian passport, both bearing the name Patrick Burke. "I still thought there was some kind of mix-up. If I hadn't seen proof from the police, I would have never believed this in a million years," she later told reporters.

Although there were those who agreed with Taylor and saw Burlakow as a nice guy who liked to stay at the best suites Seattle's Sorrento Hotel had to offer and appeared to have the means to pay cash for the $500-per-night tab, others questioned his character. In May 2003, Seattle-based KOMO 4 News unveiled another victim of Burlakow's charms. Although it's not clear when Burlakow moved from the Seattle house Taylor said he owned, or if he ever actually owned such a property, at some point, Burlakow approached George Johnson to rent a house-boat he owned. Johnson agreed to the rental, accepting a $4400 cheque from him for the first and last month's rent. "He (also) wrote the previous tenant a $2000 check for the hot tub, both of which bounced," Johnson told KOMO reporters in May 2003. "So, he came on as, he's very personable, he's a very good con-versationalist. He's charming and he snowed us."

It was becoming increasingly difficult to deny the fact that, whoever Burlakow really was, his new identity as a con man was starting to reveal itself. But Burlakow had a bit of ground to cover between his Vancouver heist and his arrest before people began to piece together his true identity.

FLASHBACK

Over the five weeks since his successful robbery in Vancouver, Burlakow hit five more banks before getting caught. On January 21, just 11 days after the Vancouver heist, Burlakow was back on his home turf, where he held up the Canadian Imperial Bank of Commerce (CIBC) on Winnipeg's Roblin Boulevard. A surveillance camera caught an image of Burlakow, and a boot print attributed to him was also discovered. By now, the once-model citizen was being touted as the "Fat Bandit," thanks to his five-foot eight-inch, 350-pound frame, and he was getting so brazen that, if he knew of the police department's findings, they didn't seem to deter him.

On January 24, only three days after the CIBC robbery, Burlakow hit another Scotiabank, this one located on Ness Avenue. This time, he scored $4869, after tossing a dye pack back at the teller who'd ignored his now-customary demand for no dye packs. Almost two weeks later, on February 5, Burlakow robbed the Cambrian Credit Union on St. Mary's Road. He walked away with $2850 in that heist but was spotted in the parking lot, and it was thought he might have been driving with stolen licence plates. Two days later, Burlakow hit another Scotiabank just down the road from the Roblin Boulevard CIBC he'd robbed just days earlier. He made off with $5123 in the hit, but a neighbour allegedly saw him changing his clothing inside his vehicle.

The beginning of the end came on Valentine's Day. With the weekend ahead, Burlakow probably thought the afternoon traffic would save him from getting caught in his last heist, should he find himself on the run from police. It was a Friday, after all. A day for sweethearts. Special days often have the effect of mellowing us out and leaving us lighthearted. As Burlakow strolled into the Scotiabank at 528 Waterloo Street, at about 2:10 in the afternoon, he did so believing he'd score another clean getaway. Unfortunately for him, but to the collective relief of Winnipeg's bank tellers, their friends and families and the men in blue, that wasn't the case. This time, the police were ready for him; they were expecting another attempted robbery.

With a combination of luck, sheer persistence and good planning, the police were on the scene moments after receiving a call that the Waterloo Street Scotiabank had been robbed, and, by all accounts, it was the same guy who'd pulled the previous robberies. The Waterloo Street robbery, however, claimed one significant difference—the robber was believed to have been armed with a semi-automatic handgun when he approached the teller and demanded money. With his bag full, Burlakow dashed outside and climbed into what witnesses said was a "black sports utility vehicle." Bristling with the possibility of finally capturing and putting the elusive "Fat Bandit" behind bars, every available police officer in the area was on the lookout for a vehicle matching witness descriptions. Shortly after Burlakow bolted, a police officer spotted what looked like the bandit's SUV and signalled the driver to pull over. But instead of complying, the driver floored the gas and darted through the busy city streets. According to one news report, Burlakow clocked speeds of up to 160 kilometres per hour before leaving the city limits through Headingly and crashing into a ditch just north of the small town of Starbuck.

Still unwilling to give up, Burlakow had to be "forced out of the SUV at gunpoint," but the bank robber who'd so suddenly appeared on the scene and hit seven banks in a matter of months was finally in handcuffs. Burlakow later said that he wasn't really trying to evade police—he was trying to call home. He wanted to give his wife and daughter some kind of explanation about why their life was about to turn upside down. Regardless of his motives, Burlakow was now on his way to getting a room courtesy of the City of Winnipeg, but, instead of a cushy suite at the Sorrento, he'd be in a cold cell, behind bars and bereft of any accoutrements. Facing nine counts of robbery, nine counts of wearing a disguise, two counts of theft under $500 and a single count each of fleeing police and dangerous driving, Burlakow was not likely to set foot in a bank any time soon. If the one-time civil servant thought life was hard after "retiring" from his job with the City and finding an adequate replacement, he was about to find that life was going to be more challenging than he could have imagined.

THE BUREAUCRAT BANDIT

Shock.

There was no other word for it. The first response from neighbours and city officials who were willing to talk about Burlakow's arrest was disbelief. Like Cathy Taylor, had the police not arrested the man and produced supporting evidence, many of those who knew Burlakow would have stood behind him, crying foul in his defence. "He was a good employee... He was dedicated. He was professional, and he knew how to handle things," Counsellor Harry Lazarenko told *Sun* reporter Cary Castagna following Burlakow's arrest.

Glen Murray, Winnipeg's mayor at the time of Burlakow's arrest, said he was "shocked and saddened" when he heard about his former employee's situation, but he was also cautious with his comments, saying the matter was before the courts. Former mayor Susan Thompson had no problem sharing her thoughts on Burlakow's arrest, however, defending Burlakow's work ethic and telling *Sun* reporter Katie Chalmers that, "Something has gone terribly wrong in his life for this to happen." Some of Burlakow's neighbours also came forward, claiming to be surprised by the news and saying they never expected this kind of behaviour from the man they knew.

But others had different opinions about Burlakow's character. Chalmers uncovered several of Burlakow's Arbor Grove neighbours, who reportedly didn't care for him. Counsellor Harvey Smith reflected on Burlakow's sudden and early retirement, saying he learned of it by email the day Burlakow was scheduled to leave, and that wasn't the usual protocol for City Hall. Although there were no public allegations that Burlakow was into anything illegal, Smith suggested that Burlakow was asked to leave after some errors were spotted in his work. However, Bob Gannon, Winnipeg's chief financial officer, was quick to defend Burlakow, saying he never knew the man to do anything questionable during his time with the City.

So, who exactly was Klaus Burlakow, and how could he have digressed to becoming a bank robber?

According to Mike Cook, Burlakow's first lawyer, the man who had terrorized the city's bank staff and customers for three months didn't suffer from substance abuse or addiction that might have led to his crime spree. Cook stopped short of commenting on Burlakow's finances and defended his client in the media, telling reporter David Schmeichel that Burlakow was distressed about his situation and that this was his first run-in with the law in his 48 years.

Burlakow's anxiety was apparent when he was denied bail on February 19; both the defendant and his family shed tears over the decision. To this point, it was likely that Burlakow still had friends and acquaintances rooting for him.

That wouldn't last long.

THE CRITICAL INCIDENT

Winnipeggers first heard Burlakow's response to his situation on February 18, 2003, four days after the Valentine's Day heist. He denied all 22 charges laid against him and appeared shocked and disoriented by his experience. "We want him to be able to return to his home and lead a productive life," Cook told reporters on behalf of his client.

Burlakow repeatedly maintained his innocence, even after he was denied bail. Instead of coming clean and providing his family, his lawyers and the entire city with a reason for suddenly snapping and embracing a criminal lifestyle, Burlakow and his lawyer were appealing the decision. But Burlakow's situation was continuing to deteriorate. He'd been named as a suspect in the Vancouver Scotiabank robbery. Details of the Vancouver heist hit the Winnipeg papers on February 20. Detective Darcy Taylor told reporters that witnesses thought they saw what looked like a handgun being used during the commission of the robbery.

It occurred to police that if Burlakow was found guilty of the Vancouver robbery, half a country away from the Winnipeg crime scene, perhaps they should contact colleagues in Saskatchewan and Alberta to see if any similar, unsolved robberies had occurred there. The idea became especially appealing when investigators learned of Cathy Taylor and Burlakow's frequent trips to Washington state. Agents in Washington began thinking that they, too, should look at unsolved cases that fit Burlakow's pattern.

Cathy Taylor's emergence threw a wrench into the case Cook was building for his defendant and provided another shock to those who knew Burlakow and his family. Could it be true that Burlakow and Taylor were business partners? Had he really woven such an elaborate story about his life? And imagine the shock his wife felt when she heard of their supposed impending divorce. When reporters called Cook to get his take on Taylor's allegations about Burlakow's questionable business dealings and his alias as Patrick Burke, Cook denied any knowledge of them. Even after Burlakow was officially charged with the Vancouver robbery, Cook stood behind his client, arguing in favour of granting Burlakow bail. Cook went on the record saying media reports of Burlakow's so-called double life were overstated, that Burlakow's family was aware of his client's business dealings in the U.S. and that they were all credible. Yet even the most fervent of supporters must have found themselves taken aback by yet another set of allegations. After all, where there's smoke, there's usually some kind of fire.

If matters weren't looking bleak enough for the City's ex-event planner, who, by now, was also being touted as the "Bureaucrat Bandit," things were about to get worse. The Cambrian Credit Union filed a civil suit, accusing Burlakow of stealing $2850 on February 5, and Winnipeg's Platinum Travel charged Burlakow with owing $9085 on unpaid travel bills.

Although he was working on addressing the charges in his upcoming bail hearing, which, following Taylor's statements in the media, necessitated some reference to his former partner's allegations, Burlakow now also faced a 20-day deadline to respond to the two civil lawsuits.

According to media reports, Burlakow admitted to knowing the Seattle woman, wanting to establish a business in Seattle, working with Taylor in the setting up of an events-planning business and to living on a rented houseboat and spending two weeks each month in Washington. He said he thought their partnership could work very well, that if he "assisted Ms. Taylor," the proceeds from that business could provide him and his family with a good source of income and that his family was fully aware of what he was doing.

What's not clear is whether Burlakow addressed the allegations that he introduced himself by his alias, that he masqueraded as an Irish war hero and that he bounced large cheques for rent. Burlakow denied using a fake driver's licence and passport. It was nothing but "poppycock," he said. Burlakow's response to his civil suit never made it into the Winnipeg papers.

It was getting harder for Burlakow to deny his situation. By now, the public was aware that when Burlakow was arrested on February 14, he had an "air pistol and a pocketful of bait money"—specially marked bills to help track bank robbers—on him. There was no way he could logically talk his way out of his involvement in the Valentine's Day heist. Still, his lawyer made a valiant effort at representing his client. In March 2003, Cook arrived at the court house with glowing character references provided by some of Burlakow's former employees and the suggestion that, though there might be a strong case against Burlakow for the February 14 robbery, the other eight charges weren't nearly so clear-cut.

Court of Queen's Bench Justice Gerald Jewers disagreed, calling Burlakow's behaviour "unpredictable." Bail was denied, and Justice Jewers adjourned the case, citing that too many unanswered questions continued to shroud the bizarre story in mystery. "There's something more to this case than we now know," Justice Jewers said.

Just two months later, Burlakow and his lawyer changed their strategy. Perhaps they both reviewed the evidence—the similarities between several of the robberies Burlakow was charged with and the firsthand accounts of the robber's actions from tellers, such as the mother who faced Burlakow and one of his make-believe guns on "Take Our Kids to Work Day"—and felt they had no choice but to do the right thing. On Thursday, May 15, Burlakow pleaded guilty to six of the nine Winnipeg robberies and the Vancouver heist.

By now, it looked as though the nine original charges were about to grow by an increment of three—Washington State Police and the FBI were looking at Burlakow for a robbery in Lynnwood as well as another two from the Puget Sound area. Those three charges were, for the time being, on hold. As for the remainder of the original 22 indictments, the court didn't proceed with the charges of fleeing from police, wearing a disguise and theft. Cook acknowledged that the Crown had a solid case in the charges to which Burlakow pleaded guilty, that it was quite likely he would have been found guilty had his client gone to trial and that his client understood his admission meant he'd be serving a lengthy sentence.

A sentencing hearing scheduled for the summer of 2003 wasn't held for Burlakow until late January 2004. This postponement was due, in part, to Mike Cook pulling himself off the case when his client failed to pay his legal fees. Once Mike Wasylin was up to speed on his new client's case, the defence attorney suggested the court impose a three- to five-year sentence for Burlakow. After all, he had admitted to using plastic guns and pistols in seven bank robberies that netted him about $33,000. Surely it was better to save the court's time and money by avoiding a lengthy and expensive trial. Burlakow was no hardened criminal, and Wasylin said his client was very sorry for his criminal outburst, "(had) no previous criminal record" and had undergone psychological testing that revealed he posed "little risk to reoffend."

Crown prosecutor Dale Harvey disagreed with the defence and asked the judge for a stiffer sentence of 10 to 12 years. The Crown argued that Burlakow wasn't a frantic father trying to protect his family but a man who'd developed a system for each of his crimes. The fact that he'd stolen a licence plate to cover his own on each occasion proved that he was cognitive of his actions and was trying to cover his tracks and prevent detection. Burlakow had worn a mask and used fake guns that, unless you were schooled in firearms, looked like the real thing, and, after his first bungled attempt at bank robbery, he had the wherewithal to demand large bills and no dye packs. Admittedly, the picture being painted was not of a man on the verge of a nervous breakdown but of one whose actions were coolly calculated and getting more brazen as he went along.

Burlakow explained his sudden break from reality by saying he'd been forced into a life of crime. The teary-eyed 49-year-old stood before Provincial Court Chief Justice Judith Webster and wove a story about a business deal gone bad and partners who were allegedly involved in organized crime, partners he refused to finger because he was supposedly so frightened of their backlash. Burlakow said these associates disappeared with $200,000 in startup funds that Burlakow had borrowed from less-than-honourable lenders, who were demanding their money back. Because Burlakow no longer had the money and hadn't developed his planned business ventures to the extent that money was coming in, a desperate Burlakow turned to robbing banks. This was the explanation he gave to the courts. And although he never gave any names, Burlakow said he was concerned that even the minimal information he had shared put his wife and children in jeopardy.

What leap of logic propelled Burlakow to think he had no other recourse than to rob a bank to repay the money isn't clear, but he stood by his version of the events. Stories about Burlakow's involvement with the sinister characters in his life would later expand slightly and include tales of how he had to "launder drug money for organized crime" between Canada and the United States. "Certainly this was a situation where rather frightening and bizarre circumstances had gotten into my life," Burlakow told the court. "It was a situation I couldn't cope with, that was quite alien to me and in the end was quite terrifying for myself and for my family."

Despite the fact that no one was injured in the execution of the robberies, the court was quick to point out that Burlakow's actions were still violent in their intention and damaging to everyone involved. Judge Webster didn't buy Burlakow's "poor me" defence. "It is difficult to see the defendant as a victim," she told the court. "The victims were the bank tellers who were terrorized."

On Wednesday, February 3, 2004, Judge Webster slammed Burlakow with what amounted to an eight-year sentence—10 years minus two for the time he'd already spent in custody. "The offences are grave...the responsibility is solely that of the offender," Judge Webster said.

The judge's decision was applauded in the media. *Winnipeg Sun* columnist Tom Brodbeck said Judge Webster understood the law and the importance of providing a deterrent for future criminals and that other judges should follow her example and "put the 'justice' back in the justice system."

If you think this is the end of the story, think again.

AND THEN THERE WAS MORE

While Burlakow's lawyer was preparing to appeal Judge Webster's sentence, Burlakow was finding himself in the midst of yet another battle. Detective Jerry Riener of the Lynnwood, Washington, police department told reporters that plans were in the works to go ahead with an arrest warrant for Burlakow, the chief suspect in a robbery that took place in Washington's Snohomish County on January 28, 2003. Riener said investigators began considering Burlakow for the robbery when they compared video footage of the man during the commission of one of his robberies with those retrieved from the bank in their unsolved case. "One of the detectives recognized the person as being very similar to the one in our bank robbery," Riener told *Sun* reporter Katie Chalmers, adding that his colleagues referred to the suspect as "dough boy" because he, too, was a portly fellow.

Although the FBI was working alongside the Lynnwood police, they were content to take their time. After all, Burlakow wasn't going anywhere for at least a few years. Once officials in the U.S. moved forward with the planned charges, Burlakow would face an extradition hearing.

The likelihood that Burlakow would face an extradition hearing grew when he was named as a suspect in another bank robbery that took place on January 13, 2003, this one in Olympia, Washington. Exactly two weeks after the Olympia robbery, a bank in Lakewood, Washington, was also robbed, and officials there were also looking at Burlakow for that heist. Again, the suspicion was based on videotaped footage of the crime. "The build of the gentleman, the shape of his head, the dickey, the hat, the leather jacket, the words he used—these things were very similar," David Soukup, one of Thurston County's senior deputy prosecuting attorneys, told *Sun* reporter Cary Castagna.

If these additional charges weren't enough to take the wind out of Burlakow's sails, things weren't looking good for his sentence appeal, either. The Court of Appeal dismissed Burlakow's application for a reduced sentence. He'd be making the medium-security Rockwood Institution his home for some time to come.

As it turned out, this wasn't such a bad thing. While in jail, Burlakow received the welcome news that he wasn't going to be extradited to the U.S., after all. In February 2006, reports hit the newspapers that Burlakow's lawyer had managed to assuage the fears of American prosecutors, no doubt using the psychological profile conducted on Burlakow to convince them that his client wasn't likely to reoffend. That, along with telling U.S. officials that Burlakow had been behaving himself in jail and only committed his crimes under "great duress," appeared to produce positive results—at least, as far as Burlakow and his lawyer were concerned.

American authorities might have thought twice about their decision had they known Burlakow's eight-year sentence was about to be considerably reduced.

Canadian Justice Too Soft?

Winnipeg residents first learned that their now infamous ex-civil servant turned bank robber was about to get day parole on September 26, 2006, after serving only two and a half years of an eight-year sentence. Although Judge Webster didn't fall for Burlakow's sob story, a parole board panel was ready to give him the benefit of the doubt. During his time in jail, Burlakow was thought to be a model prisoner and was still considered "a low risk to re-offend." In a written statement, the panel reviewing the bandit's case said they believed Burlakow understood that when he conducted his crimes he was "in a spiral of self-destructive behaviour." As soon as a bed in a halfway house was available, Burlakow would be back in the community, doing just about anything anyone else could do, as long as he followed the rules.

The announcement stunned the community, with some residents shaking their heads and suggesting that this was yet another case of having two sets of laws—one for the "bigwigs," such as Burlakow and other officials, and one for the rest of society. Burlakow's story was once again fuel for Tom Brodbeck's column. He warned readers that it was a small step from day parole to full parole and that Burlakow would be eligible for full parole after serving a third of his sentence, which translated into 32 months or just a few months after receiving his day parole. "When you put him back on the street after serving only two and a half years (of an eight-year sentence), you're not easing him back into society, you're just letting him out early—probably to save money," Brodbeck wrote.

In any case, the wheels of justice ticked along fairly smoothly for the Bureaucrat Bandit. To be fair, at first, Burlakow seemed to blend in quite nicely with society; he kept clean, as far as anyone knew, and even landed himself a pretty good job. In fact, he was behaving himself so well that, on April 19, 2007, Burlakow received full parole and was as good as a free man. Yes, he'd have to live with the good folks of the Correctional Service of Canada checking up on him now and again until February 3, 2012, when the full term of his sentence was completed, but Burlakow could live with that. He was just glad he wasn't behind bars anymore and had no intention of returning to jail. Burlakow had been planning for his release from the moment he was incarcerated. The first order of business in his fresh, new life was to secure a name change—he no longer liked the kind of notoriety that came with the name Klaus Burlakow. To be honest, he never liked his name. "Klaus Dieter Burlakow. How does that sound to you? I'll tell you how it sounds to me.

Ethnic. I can't think of a worse name," he told *Globe and Mail* correspondent Susan Bourette. "This is a white, Anglo-Saxon town, and if you're not old money—if you're not part of that old boys network—you'll never get anywhere. That was part of the desire to change my name."

He'd completed the name change before his release; Timothy Michael Collins had such a nice ring to it, the surname "Collins" of good Anglo-Saxon origin with just a hint of Irish and maybe even a little Gaelic in its heritage. Perhaps he'd even dig up the Irish brogue he'd practiced on Cathy Taylor. But he'd worry about that later. Right now, he had a job to find, and he had a few ideas.

Although he wouldn't return to the wife and kids and the homelife he'd had before his incarceration, Burlakow continued to make strides in rebuilding his life. While still in prison, he'd gotten involved with the program Open Circle, the Mennonite Central Committee's (MCC) prisoner visitation program. The program's philosophy is that crime destroys relationships and distances a criminal from his or her family, friends and community, and being behind bars only pushes the incarcerated individual into deeper isolation. Overall, the prognosis for rehabilitation under these circumstances is far from optimal. Open Circle's volunteers try to rebuild some sense of community for criminals and encourage healing, by befriending them and walking alongside them on their journey. Burlakow told reporters that the program, and in particular the volunteer assigned to him, changed his life and helped him believe in himself again. Once he was released, Burlakow continued working with some of the people he'd met through Open Circle.

Burlakow must have impressed the MCC volunteers as much as they had impressed him, because, in the spring of 2008, he landed full-time employment as a consultant and fundraising manager for a new MCC project called Sam's Place. Spokesperson Brad Reimer went on record saying that, for the most part, the people there had no problem working with the ex-convict and that Burlakow had volunteered and remained involved with MCC from the time he was released from prison. "He has never hidden the fact of who he is or what he's done," Reimer told reporters.

After working with an MCC advisory committee on the Sam's Place project, Burlakow, it was clear, had a skill set that would prove invaluable to the organization. When applications for the position of project manager were being accepted, Burlakow applied through his new company, Blackrose Solutions. And when he landed the job, he was quick to share how he felt about it with the media. "It's an honour to work for people who care so much about other people," he told reporters.

Sam's Place, a new café and bookshop at 159 Henderson Highway, was scheduled to open in the fall of 2008 but held its grand opening in April 2009. The cozy coffee shop was a new venture for the Christian organization. The seed for the idea came when someone mentioned how sad it was to see so many books left over from MCC relief sales, which are held as a fund-raiser for MCC projects, and that it would be a great idea to have a permanent place to sell these leftover books. The idea of opening a used-book store blossomed into one of establishing a place that, as board member Dan Block said during the official opening, "would become a centre of community activity" for the residents of Elmwood. Along with thousands of books, food and refreshments would be available as well as a stage for nightly entertainment. The proceeds from sales would go to MCC programs. Sam's Place, named for the café's mascot—a Komodo dragon of the same name—was supposed to be a warm, safe place for folks to gather.

As project manager, Burlakow was responsible for overseeing the establishment of the new home for this "one-of-a-kind-project." In this capacity, he'd have to make financial decisions and was essentially the man at the helm of a $300,000 renovation project. But MCC staff was quick to point out that everything Burlakow did, especially when it came to spending money, would be guided and approved by the board. And, although some questioned the wisdom of a man with Burlakow's past heading such a large venture, others fully supported the decision.

Despite the mixture of emotions at MCC over his hiring, Burlakow seemed to have performed his duties reasonably well during his tenure at Sam's Place. He even landed a front-page story in the April issues of two Mennonite publications, *Canadian*

Mennonite and *Mennonite Weekly Review*. The articles praised his efforts in creating Sam's Place and gave Burlakow a chance to share what he thought about his good fortune. "I believe in second chances, not only for myself, but for everyone," he told reporters. "If you have a sincere desire to live a good life, you should be given the opportunity to do that. Everyone deserves a chance for redemption." And, indeed, Burlakow seemed to have every intention of rehabilitating himself.

At least, for a while.

SAME SONG, DIFFERENT VERSE

Just when Burlakow was getting used to some positive press, the headlines turned sour again. Only a month after he was praised in Canada's Mennonite media circles and lifted up as a success story for Open Circle, the words "Con artist sent back to prison" screamed across the pages of the May 20, 2009, issue of the *Winnipeg Free Press*. According to the story written by Bruce Owen and Mike McIntyre, Burlakow was sent back to Stony Mountain Institution because of parole violations stemming from "questionable financial transactions" that occurred since his release from prison. The story explained that Burlakow had provided a woman named Rosie Neufeld with promissory notes for $9500, plus interest, but hadn't come through with the money, even after selling his house. When Burlakow didn't show up in court to address these issues, along with another claim for $949.45 from CDC Installation Systems for work the company claimed was completed at his house and hadn't been paid for, he was found in default. Although Burlakow didn't appear to address the charges and was ordered to pay the debts, at least one of the individuals involved suggested Burlakow didn't follow through with that order. That's when one of Neufeld's associates apparently contacted the parole board.

Not surprisingly, a visibly upset Burlakow denied any criminal wrongdoing. As far as he was concerned, the only thing he could be accused of was putting blind faith in the wrong people, in this case, the Neufelds, who had told Burlakow they were planning to set up some type of equestrian centre or professional rodeo grounds. In a July 2009 interview, Burlakow told Owen that the lion's share of Neufeld's claim, $8000 of it, was actually payment for a promotional plan and PowerPoint presentation that Burlakow put together for the project. It was allegedly money the couple had struggled to pay and wanted returned when the venture fell through. "I could ostensibly be sitting in here for nearly two years not having done anything, committing no crimes, doing nothing other than making a very bad business decision to ever get involved with (these people)... I will confess that I should have never got involved with them," Burlakow said.

MCC's Russ Loewen cautiously spoke on the matter, telling Dean Pritchard of the *Winnipeg Sun* that, although Burlakow and Sam's Place had parted ways on April 9, MCC had nothing but good things to say about his performance.

"Tim did a good job to get (Sam's Place) up and running and through mutual agreement he moved on to something else.... We did not go to the police or to his parole officer with anything." Loewen reinforced the group's support of Burlakow, telling the *Canadian Mennonite* that they had not fired him, as some media reports indicated.

Semantics aside, the public was getting enough information on Burlakow's most recent escapades to question whether he was really as rehabilitated as some officials seemed to suggest. In addition to the roughly $12,000 the courts said he owed and was allegedly remiss in paying back, Burlakow had apparently struck up a relationship with a 50-year-old Kentucky woman. According to one story, the woman had contacted the *Free Press* to ask about the man she said she knew as Collins when she'd lost touch with him. She said she met Collins on a "social networking site" and that they had developed a relationship, even visiting each other in Toronto, Ottawa and Halifax. She explained that they'd fallen in love and planned to get married; she'd even paid for a house inspection on a home the couple were thinking of buying in Atlanta, at a time when visiting Atlanta would have been a violation of his probation. Moving to the American city was certainly out of the question—some sources suggested that the woman's story, should it prove to be true, implied that Burlakow was thinking of skipping town and reneging on the money he owed. Burlakow avoided commenting on the accusations.

Although Burlakow was back in the clink, reporters were still scrambling to find more newsworthy information on the con man. The *Canadian Mennonite*, a national biweekly magazine, discovered that, although MCC was standing behind their man, the company had two garnishee orders on Burlakow. *Canadian Mennonite* managing editor Ross W. Muir broke the story, and, although MCC officials were hesitant to comment, Muir discovered that a "notice of garnishment for $3630 was filed (against Burlakow) under the name 'Mennonite Central Committee' on October 30, 2008," and another "$3710 was filed under the name 'Sam's Place Board' on April 6, 2009." Any further explanations regarding these orders were never made public. Suffice it to say that Burlakow's life in the last decade has been anything but boring.

Despite the public fallout over Burlakow's situation and being called to defend their position on hiring him as Sam's Place manager, a move that complies with their mandate as it's explained in Matthew 25:36, "I was in prison and you visited me...a stranger and you welcomed me," Open Circle continues to reach out to prisoners and pray for their rehabilitation. MCC Manitoba's constituency relations department spokesperson Brad Reimer went on record with *Canadian Mennonite*, backing the group's decision to hire Burlakow and saying there was no conflict of interest in his hiring. "I think this particular circumstance was one of both not having other applicants and wanting to give Mr. Collins a chance. If this is not 'best business practice,' then maybe it is 'best Christian practice.'"

Peter Remple, MCC's executive director, echoed that belief. In a prepared statement, he said, "MCC has reached out to offenders in various ways for several decades on the basis of our belief that God can and does help people who have committed crimes." Before his parole was revoked, Burlakow seemed like a poster child for MCC's efforts. He admitted to having had "a huge fall from grace," and that he'd "lost his moral compass." Through the kind folks at MCC and the Open Circle program, Burlakow said that he came to understand that the "Christian ethic revolves around forgiveness, redemption and second chances." Sadly, like most con artists, Burlakow, it seems, learned everything he could about the people who were reaching out to him, only to turn around and take advantage of their good graces.

THE LATEST CHAPTER

On July 15, 2009, Burlakow caught the second big break of his life when the National Parole Board reinstated his full parole status. In their judgment, the National Parole Board called Burlakow's business dealings "unwise" but not "illegal." His actions would be under close scrutiny, however. "The board is concerned with your judgment regarding business transactions, and any similar behaviour may lead to revocation (of his parole)."

As of this writing, Burlakow appears to have kept himself out of the spotlight. Stories of his exploits quieted down in the months following his rerelease into society. But Google his name—either Klaus Burlakow or Timothy Michael Collins—and you'll discover he's still apt to make news on various Internet chat sites. Discussions about his alleged antics take up several pages of the Winnipeg Forum, an Internet message board "for and about Winnipeggers." In this chat room, contributors have let off steam, sharing their thoughts and alleged experiences about Burlakow, but the information isn't all verified, and much of it is speculative. Warnings about Burlakow are also posted at www.ripoffreport.com, although much of the information on this site comprises postings of past newspaper articles.

As individuals accusing Burlakow of victimizing them continue to trickle out of the woodwork, the Bureaucrat Bandit has been immortalized in two books and a song. Yes, he's more of a bumbling Keystone Cop–type figure than a Billy the Kid, but fans of the Winnipeg-based "rock n' roll terrorist squad," Hot Live Guys, won't forget him any time soon—he's the subject of their popular song, "Robbin' a Bank." Where the roller coaster that is Burlakow's life will take him during his remaining years, only time will tell. But for now, he's an example of what at least some Winnipeg residents have believed all along—you can't trust a bureaucrat.

Chapter Six

Show Me the Money

Cassie L. Chadwick

~

*[Mr. Carnegie] expressed not a little surprise at the
gullibility of some persons. He repeated his many previous assertions that he did not know the woman at all,
had never known her and in fact left the impression
that he did not care to make her acquaintance now that
he had managed to escape further annoyance without
knowing her.*

–Director Edward Bigelow, Department of Public Works,
sharing a conversation he had with Andrew Carnegie about
Ms. Cassie Chadwick with the *New York Times*,
December 28, 1904

What Is Truth?

For some people, there's no such thing as a lie. That way,
you never have to worry about keeping your stories
straight. What you communicate at this moment is true
for this moment. It may not be true for tomorrow—tomorrow
will no doubt have its own truth.

The concept might make your head spin, but it's about the best way to explain Cassie L. Chadwick, the stories she wove in and about her life and the web of illusions she spun for historians trying to write about her. From the information available, it's hard to assess if she actually meant to lie or if, at some point during her lifetime, she came to believe her lies, even when they contradicted each other. Either way, she appeared fearless in her pursuits and didn't seem to have a stop button when it came to satisfying her personal desires.

WELCOME TO THE WORLD!

Cassie L. Chadwick was born Elizabeth Bigley on October 10—historians agree on her birth name and the day and month she was born. What year she was born isn't clear: sources list it as 1856, 1857 and 1859, though the year on her gravestone is apparently 1857. Exactly where she was born is also a matter of debate, but most sources agree she made her grand entry into this world in Eastwood, Ontario, a small community just east of Woodstock.

By all accounts, Cassie was a mischievous child who was full of energy, had an eye for pretty things and loved to dream big. She had three sisters and a brother, and, according to one source, even her siblings commented that Cassie stretched the truth to get what she wanted.

Cassie's first public attempt to get her hands on something that wasn't hers came at the age of 14. She conned a farmer out of $250, earning herself a night in jail for the deed. Another story describes a young Cassie opening a bank account, allegedly using a "letter of inheritance" from an English uncle who'd recently passed away. Once the account was opened, she went shopping, writing cheques for her purchases. Of course, the cheques bounced, the merchants lost their money and Cassie was in trouble. She was arrested on charges of forgery but didn't spend any time behind bars. Apparently, the courts took her age into account (some accounts say she was in her early twenties; others suggest she was quite a bit younger), and at least one source suggested the courts labelled her "insane."

Small-town Ontario just didn't do it for the budding con woman. If she wanted to take care of herself properly, she'd have to seek centres whose men had deeper pockets. And so, Cassie moved to Toronto and then to London, where she purportedly worked in a brothel for a time.

Eventually, Cassie made her way to Cleveland, Ohio, on the heels of her recently married sister, Alice, and Alice's husband, Bill York. Cassie only stayed with them a short while, but it was long enough to provide her with equity on a loan—she used her sister's furniture as collateral to back her newest business venture as a clairvoyant. By the time Alice discovered the deception, Cassie was living on her own and had opened for business. Until that time, she went by her birth name, Elizabeth, or the short form of Betsy, but, as a clairvoyant, she needed something more mysterious, so she took the name Madame Lydia de Vere.

About this time, Cassie met up with Dr. Wallace S. Springsteen and, working her charms on the young man, finagled a proposal. The two married on November 21, 1882. For a grand total of 11 days, Cassie was known as Mrs. Wallace Springsteen, until her new husband discovered her checkered past and asked her to leave. The short marriage cost him a considerable amount of money—he wound up paying for Cassie's fraudulently acquired loan, as well as other debts she'd accumulated. The couple's divorce was finalized early the following year.

With or without a husband, Cassie clearly had to bring in some money if she was to continue living in the way to which she'd become accustomed; as Madame Marie LaRose (other renditions of her story suggest she simply resurrected her earlier alias of Madame Lydia de Vere) she was again offering her skill at fortune-telling. She'd tell anyone just about anything they wanted to know—for a price.

Around 1886 or 1887, not long after her divorce, and some time after re-establishing her fortune-telling business, Cassie met Ohio farmer John R. Scott. He and Cassie tied the knot—but not before she had him sign a prenuptial agreement. She'd had it drawn up because of the abuse she said she suffered at the hands of her first husband. Life seemed almost normal, though it wasn't for long. Four years later, Cassie filed for divorce, took every financial advantage she could from her latest husband and returned to clairvoyance.

For a time, she worked as Lydia Scott then as Madame LaRose, but taking money from innocent people who believed in her alleged fortune-telling abilities wasn't enough. She wanted more money, and she wanted it faster than it was coming in, so she again turned to forgery. Cassie was living in Toledo when the authorities caught up with her in 1889 for perpetrating a $10,000 scam. This time, she didn't get off without paying her dues—she was sentenced to nine and a half years in a Toledo jail.

Few criminals complete their entire sentence behind bars; four years later, Cassie was paroled and by 1894 was living in Cleveland again. There was no mention of the man she supposedly married, but Cassie had assumed the name Mrs. Cassie Hoover and passed herself off as a widow—if there was a marriage, it, too, had ended.

As the widow Mrs. Hoover, Cassie opened a brothel, keeping a close watch on her girls and their clients. It can only be assumed that she was scouting for potential husband number four when, several years after opening her thriving business, she met Dr. Leroy Chadwick. The gentleman doctor was in mourning, having just lost his wife of many years, and when Cassie met him, she told him she was running a "respectable boarding house for women" and "teaching etiquette" to the ladies. Leroy Chadwick likely had a chuckle at her expense, telling her that everyone knew the place was a brothel. Playing her character to the fullest, Cassie fainted at the news. One story describes how she endeared herself to the widowed doctor, and, when she regained consciousness, she begged him to take her away from that wretched place; had she known, she would never have lowered herself to being seen anywhere near that kind of establishment. Chadwick apparently bought her story. He complied with her wishes, and by 1897 the two were married.

THE CHADWICK AFFAIR

Until she met Leroy, Cassie's scams had been pretty small. She was a con woman, no doubt, and she likely tried to scam everyone she met. But when she married Leroy, she must have thought she'd hit pay dirt. The Chadwicks were an old, established family in Cleveland, and the home she shared with Leroy located on Euclid Avenue, which the locals called "Millionaire's Row" and the rest of the country called "the most beautiful street in America," was as stately as it was beautiful. In her wildest dreams, she couldn't have imagined living in such elegance, and, because her husband was so popular, Cassie—despite her sometimes odd behaviour—was included in his friends' high-society activities.

Despite her newfound wealth, Cassie's appetite for spending never seemed satisfied. Playing the role of fortune-teller certainly wouldn't do for a society woman. Neither would running a brothel. No, this time, Cassie concocted a scam that was far more elaborate and far more lucrative than either of her previous moneymaking schemes.

In the late 1890s, New York City was still a budding metropolis. By 1877, Currier & Ives had already immortalized the Brooklyn Bridge in the print entitled *The Great East River Suspension Bridge*. By 1898, Manhattan, the Bronx, Brooklyn, Queens and Staten Island had consolidated to form the five boroughs of New York City. And by the time Cassie L. Chadwick paid her first visit to what would one day be called the Big Apple, one of the country's most innovative entrepreneurs and most generous philanthropists was making his home there for at least part of every year. It was time, Cassie reasoned, that she paid Mr. Andrew Carnegie of the Carnegie Steel Company a short but well-thought-out visit.

During a trip to New York, Cassie asked a lawyer acquaintance of hers by the name of James Dillon to drive her to Carnegie's home. She was secretive about the reasons behind her request, and she spent a considerable length of time inside the mansion. According to one source, Cassie posed as a wealthy New Yorker looking for a reference for a maid she was thinking of hiring—the maid had said she once worked for Carnegie. She didn't readily offer up any more information when she returned to the car, but, as she climbed into the vehicle, she let slip a piece of paper. Dillon picked up the paper and was surprised to find that it looked like a promissory note signed by Carnegie himself. Swearing Dillon to secrecy, Cassie explained that she'd contacted

Carnegie some time ago, introducing herself as his illegitimate daughter, and he'd since provided her with promissory notes totalling $7 million, with a further promise that she'd inherit his $400 million fortune.

Of course, the best thing about a secret is telling someone, and, after the lawyer helped Cassie establish a safety deposit box to safely house her promissory notes, the juicy gossip she'd just shared leaked out. Before she knew it, she was being offered one loan after another. Banks fought to get her business. Lending Chadwick large sums of money at exorbitant interest rates would make them plenty.

Now she wasn't just living on Millionaire's Row, she was living the life of a millionaire. Over the next several years, she continued to borrow money against the promissory notes locked away in her safety deposit box, spending it on diamonds and clothes and the best hats you could buy. There appeared to be no end to the gullible people in high-powered positions who believed her story, and no end to the banks knocking at her door. There was very little chance her con would ever get discovered. After all, who was brazen enough to walk up to Carnegie and ask him if he had an illegitimate daughter?

And then, just as quickly as she'd been catapulted into the highlife and dubbed the "Queen of Ohio," the teller doors slammed shut. Herbert B. Newton, a banker from Boston, Massachusetts, called in his loan of $190,000. One story describes how Newton learned, through the grapevine, of the large amounts of money Cassie had been borrowing, and the news disturbed him. Cassie's loan through Newton's bank was fairly new—she'd just received it in November 1904. Still, the banker thought it was better to collect what she owed him now than to wait and face a possible loss.

Having never been confronted by any of the banks she'd been conning, Cassie was shocked. She couldn't believe the nerve—it was as if, by then, she believed her own rhetoric and thought it impertinent of the banker to bother her with such a petty request. Cassie certainly believed she'd be inheriting the Carnegie fortune. All she had to do was survive the old man who, by that time, was already well into his 60s. She had every expectation that she'd outlive him and that she'd be able to prove beyond a shadow of a doubt that the promissory notes in her possession were authentic.

Of course, they weren't.

FACING THE MUSIC

It didn't take long for news of Newton's concerns to filter into the other banking institutions that had loaned Cassie money. Pretty soon, everyone was asking questions, and when Andrew Carnegie was finally approached about his relationship to Cassie L. Chadwick, he obviously denied knowing anything about her. That, of course, rang alarm bells through the banking institutions intimately aware of Cassie.

On December 12, 1904, the *New York Times* reported that the "Queen of Ohio" had been indicted on one count of forging and one count of "uttering forged paper." The charges stemmed from two separate notes, both related to Carnegie—one for $250,000 and another for $500,000.

While Cassie was dealing with the authorities, and the press, her doctor husband was purportedly in Paris, France, avoiding all the commotion. Cassie went on record, saying she'd spoken with him, that he backed her all the way and believed in her innocence. Despite all the hoopla, Cassie was the picture of confidence. As her train from New York pulled into the Cleveland station, media reported that an estimated 10,000 people were waiting for her to emerge. Their presence, however, wasn't so much a sign of support as a show of disgust. "Hisses, hoots, catcalls and jeers greeted her instead of expressions of sympathy," the *New York Times* reported on December 15, 1904. "As the unhappy woman alighted from her car, the crowd surged forward as though to mob her, and only by desperate efforts were the police able to hold it back."

Although visibly shaken by the experience, Cassie got herself together and defended herself in the *New York Times*:

> *I am an honest woman…assure my friends and those who believe in me that I will not disappoint the confidence they repose in me. I will show them and the whole world that I am an honest woman; that I have never wrongfully obtained money from any one and*

that I will repay every dollar of my indebtedness. For the next two or three days I will consider the important matters to which I referred and will decide on my attorney. Then I will plan my fight for freedom and for the re-establishment of my good name.

Over the next several months, Cassie ruled the print media, but instead of being referred to as the "Queen of Ohio," she was dubbed "Cleveland's most famous con artist," a title she still holds.

On March 11, 1905, Cassie Chadwick was found guilty on seven counts of fraud. On March 27, she learned her fate—10 years in prison. Her lawyer appealed, but the appeal was denied. The Ohio Penitentiary would be her home for the next decade.

She never got out alive. On her birthday, October 10, 1907, Cassie Chadwick died in prison. No family was by her bedside, although, following her death, it became public knowledge that she had a son named Emil from her first marriage. He had been sent for but didn't arrive in time to see his mother before she passed away.

POSTSCRIPT

Although only one reference even remotely connected Dr. Chadwick with his wife's scams, that being a brief mention that he was with her when she placed a promissory note in her safety deposit box, at one point, the doctor found himself being confronted by the authorities. There was some concern that he might have been involved in his wife's frauds. Those concerns must have been addressed, because an article in the March 22, 1905, edition of the *New York Times* announced that Dr. Chadwick agreed to play the $9000 organ that once belonged to his wife and was now the property of Abram Nelson of New Market. The organ was among the items sold from the Chadwick estate. Chadwick would be paid $100 per week for his services: a story about the agreement appeared in the *New York Times*, explaining that Chadwick would be doing this for Nelson wherever the organ was placed on public display.

Cassie apparently did have accomplices. Charles Beckwith and A.B. Spear, president and cashier, respectively, of a National Bank in Oberlin, Ohio, one of those Cassie had targeted, were both charged with breaking various banking laws. Beckwith died before going to trial, and Spear pleaded guilty.

Exactly how much money Cassie scammed over the years was never accurately ascertained, but it was estimated at between $2 million and $20 million. When she died, her body was interred in Woodstock, Ontario.

This is not the end.

On October 19, 1907, the *New York Times* revived the Cassie Chadwick fraud story with big headlines: "Chadwick funds in banks." Apparently, Cassie was planning for her release and still had in excess of $300,000 tucked away.

Unfortunately, she never saw a penny.

Chapter Seven

Playing with Fire

ALEXANDER (SANDY) KEITH,
A.K.A. WILLIAM KING THOMPSON ET AL

~

Men have sometimes been ready to sacrifice the lives of
many innocent people in order to accomplish the death
of some hated person; wreckers have lured ships on dan-
gerous reefs by showing false lights, and desperate villains
have thrown trains from the rails for purposes of plunder.
But none of these plots, bad as they were, contemplated
such a wholesale slaughter as this.

—*New York Times* commentary on the Dynamite Fiend,
December 17, 1875

B lack. Everything was black. Days wore on in an agoniz-
ing and unspeakable monotony that produced more
darkness than light. Moans and groans from the dying,
the maimed, the scorched and scared echoed throughout the
streets of Bremerhaven; you didn't have to be nearby to hear
them—their cries reverberated in memory and imagination. And
if you hadn't witnessed the carnage from the largest explosion the

area had ever experienced, word pictures of the disaster were vivid enough. Scarcely a family hadn't been touched, in some way, by what had taken place in the city's harbour that December 11, 1875. Scarcely a soul hadn't heard the story and shaken his head in anger, disgust and sympathy. Friends, family and healthcare workers gathered at bedsides, comforting loved ones and trying their best to ease their pain. But, pacing near the bed on which the man known as William King Thompson lay his bruised and swollen head, Louis Castan merely waited for the man to die: Thompson, the man responsible for the explosion, was not long for this world.

Castan didn't know Thompson before the two bullets had penetrated the man's skull—the two men would likely have walked in very different circles throughout their lives, although they shared at least one common interest. Like Thompson, Castan was a businessman looking for an opportunity to pad his bank account. As the owner and manager of the Panopticum, a popular Berlin wax museum of the day, Castan was sketching and making notes in preparation for the mould he was planning to take of Thompson's head once he died. A wax bust of such a notorious man would surely attract customers. Castan knew it would.

Dr. Soldan, a Bremerhaven physician, was also checking in regularly. The good doctor had received the go-ahead, on Thompson's death, to slice through the man's neck, separate his head from the rest of his body and follow up with a detailed examination of the skull. Ostensibly, the remarkable decision was made for study purposes; everyone wanted to know what could have propelled a seemingly sweet and jolly, Santa-type fellow to commit such a heinous crime against his fellow men. The question lingered—was he insane? Perhaps such drastic measures could answer that question.

According to one school of thought at the time, examining the skull and its various protrusions would provide a kind of map to understanding a person's psyche. For example, a broad, well-developed forehead, such as William Thompson had, was thought to suggest an intelligent individual; certain characteristics found behind one's ear could indicate a propensity toward greed and other unseemly behaviours. It was a theory that engendered more questions than it provided answers. Soldan must have recognized that; after all, if bumps and indentations could suggest a devious personality, then almost anyone with a motive for murder would never be held responsible for their actions. But Soldan would perform the duties expected of him, and, when Thompson was dead, he'd preserve the macabre specimen in a solution of alcohol and donate it to the city's museum.

Investigators were not only at a loss in developing a clear understanding of Thompson's psyche but also weren't any closer to identifying him. All they knew of the dying man was that he called himself William King Thompson, that he had tried to kill himself shortly after his wicked plans went awry and that he had a wife and children somewhere. Surely, Thompson's wife would have the information needed to fill in the gaps—or perhaps she was an accomplice in his dastardly deed.

Within days of the explosion, with Thompson hanging onto this world by a thread, the good Mrs. Thompson was contacted and called for under the guise of a letter from her husband. Distraught by the sudden call to her husband's side and overwhelmed with worry at his well-being, Cecelia couldn't imagine what was the matter. She hadn't heard the news—she must have been one of the very few who didn't know about the tragedy, the casualties and her husband's attempt to take his own life.

Cecelia arranged childcare for her children and arrived in Bremerhaven to face the police. After she was interrogated, prodded for information and cornered at every turn, investigators concluded that, although Cecelia might have suspected that her husband wasn't completely truthful about everything in his life during their relatively happy 10 years together, she wasn't complicit in his crimes.

Cecelia saw her husband shortly before he died; she stroked his face, held his hand and told him of her undying love and how desperately their children needed him. She read him the kindly worded letter she'd written and, after hearing the accusations against him, begged Thompson to tell the police everything he knew. But Thompson spurned her efforts, discarded her affection. To his very last breath, his words were nothing more than a purée of fact and fiction. Perhaps, by then, he didn't really know who he was. Or perhaps he believed so completely in the image of the man he made himself out to be that segments of other people's stories became his own, and he was increasingly unable to distinguish between fantasy and reality. And really, to be a successful con man, isn't that almost a prerequisite?

IN THE BEGINNING

The man who, in 1875, police knew as William King Thompson, or some variation thereof, was born Alexander Keith on November 13, 1827, in a Halkirk parish in the north of Scotland, the first child of John and Christian Keith. Named for his uncle, Alexander, and later nicknamed "Sandy" because of his hair colour, the young lad was observant and cunning. He'd watched his family adjust to changes in the agricultural way of life they were accustomed to in Scotland and witnessed the decline in his grandfather's power and the loss of his position as a tacksman (a class of landholder) and gentleman farmer.

When Sandy was nine, he and his family sailed across the Atlantic, following John's older brother and Sandy's name-sake, Alexander, to Canada. It had been more than a decade since John and Alexander had seen each other. John and his elder brother were the youngest sons of Donald Keith; they were the boys with itchy feet and a desire to look for better opportunities in greener pastures where they believed land, and success, was plentiful and accessible to anyone who worked hard. Alexander had braved the Atlantic as soon as he'd earned himself a trade as a brewmaster. He was just 21 when he landed in Halifax, took a job at Charles Boggs' brewery and began remaking himself in Canadian society.

John took a little longer to make the big decision to leave the family home and emigrate to Canada. By the time he and his family landed in the New World, Alexander Sr. was not just a well-established brewmaster, he was a businessman who, within a few years of his arrival, had put away enough cash to buy the brewery at which he'd been employed. He set about putting his own stamp on his new business, adopting as his motto the three red stags' heads of ancient Scottish mythology and producing prime ginger wine, beer and ale for the thirsty men in his midst. But it wasn't just as businessman and brewmaster that Alexander Sr. made his mark. Soon after arriving in Halifax, he entered the world of local politics. He also established his name in banking and other commercial ventures. And he garbed himself in the role of Scottish patriarch, welcoming immigrants from Scotland to this rustic new land and often lending them money when necessary. Alexander Sr. was also a central figure in the social life of the town, bringing traditional Scottish celebrations to his chosen homeland. He was the Grand Provincial Master of area Masonic lodges and was the chief of what was known as the Caledonia Club. There was no doubt as to the elder Alexander's success.

John and his family took a house a few blocks from Alexander Keith's brewery. John more than likely had expectations of a promising future, but though Alexander Sr. thrived in his chosen environment and grew wealthier with each passing year, John struggled to eke out a living for himself and his growing family. Young Sandy was observant enough to notice the socio-economic discrepancy between his father and uncle; when he came of age and the time came for him to leave school and obtain gainful employment, instead of joining his father in business, Sandy went to work for his namesake. The move must have been a tremendous blow to John, who had set up a brewery business of his own and would have very likely appreciated any assistance he could get. But his son had other plans—plans that, on closer examination, hinted at the man he'd someday become.

Long before the disaster at Bremerhaven, before some historians touted him as the "father of modern terrorism," Sandy was busy building an image for himself. He began by adding "Jr." or "the Younger" to his birth name to more closely align himself with his uncle. He began working at his uncle's brewery bottling beer but soon, after cutting himself in a serious work-place accident, started making his way up the ladder. He took on the job as company clerk and even bought shares in the business. With every effort, Sandy tried to make himself indispensable to his uncle; perhaps he thought he was.

Alexander "the Younger" also began to understand how, in many ways, his uncle was a self-made man. Sandy knew the origin of the Keith family lineage; he was aware of his family's moderate existence in Scotland. He also understood that although his uncle had created a new, more affluent life in this young country by working hard, he had also embraced, lived and believed in the role he'd adopted for himself.

It was a lesson Sandy learned well; the young Keith also set a path for himself and became his own self-made man—but the path he chose inevitably meant taking shortcuts to a life of wealth and affluence. His was an exciting life, dominated by adventure and danger, but it was a life in which the greater the chances he took, the larger the reward he'd reap. One doesn't need a roadmap, however, to know that some shortcuts aren't always on the up and up.

Although he played at being his uncle's son, Sandy knew his place in the grand scheme of things. Alexander Keith's own son, Donald, though not as adept at the family business as Alexander Jr. considered himself to be, would inherit the family brewery and the family fortune when the time came. Sandy, however, would never be more than a well-paid family employee. It was only a matter of time before he found himself kowtowing to his cousin. It was clear he would have to start padding his own bank account, making his own business connections and building a name for himself, before it was too late and he found himself just scraping by like his less-successful father.

Initially, Sandy's simple plots and ploys involved little more than basic fraud. He forged his uncle's signature on bills and other documents, and he ran a small scheme with a local grocery and liquor-store owner. It wasn't until he developed a scheme involving his position managing contracts and supplying explosives for the Halifax-to-Windsor railway project, a project the senior Keith was invested of, that the lengths to which Sandy would go to lift himself into his desired station in life became clear.

GUILTY AS SIN

One of Sandy's main responsibilities as a manager in the railway construction project was to sell and deliver gunpowder to contractors, who were blasting through the untamed wilderness in an effort to clear land for the laying of track. At regular intervals, Sandy manoeuvred his wagon up to the Halifax magazine, located near the city's waterfront. There, he'd pack a load of gunpowder, pay the magazine's manager and bring the explosives to workers along the railway line. On behalf of the investors footing the bill for the project, Sandy was paying the Halifax magazine 25 cents per pound and reselling the gunpowder to the contractors at the same price. To all outward appearances, the exchange was above-board, but as the project went on, the investors became suspicious—perhaps the supply of explosives at the Halifax magazine failed to match the amount of gunpowder that should have been needed for the railway job. Was it possible that Sandy was buying the gunpowder from another supplier, one offering the goods at half the price? This would be a wonderful thing for the investors—if Sandy was passing those savings along. The problem was that Sandy continued to charge the Halifax price, and investors began to suspect he was pocketing the difference.

Catching wind of their suspicions, and knowing they were true, Sandy had to move quickly or his get-rich-quick scheme would soon be discovered. If that happened, Sandy would not only find himself in trouble with the law, but he'd also have a lot of cheated businessmen coming after him and demanding their money back—money that Sandy more than likely had already spent on his increasingly lavish lifestyle. The crooked entrepreneur knew that, at some point, an inventory of the Halifax magazine would be organized and the proof needed to confront him on his dishonest scheme collected.

Faced with the urgent need to conceal his wrongdoing, Sandy devised a way to cover up the discrepancy—he'd blow up the evidence. And on a hot August night in 1857, just as Halifax residents were bedding down for the night, a massive explosion rocked the city. Were it not for the human carnage, the cries and wails of people whose limbs had been stripped from their bodies, their skin burned and their faces cut and scorched by flying glass and burning debris, the brilliantly lit sky might have been a wonder to behold. But there was nothing attractive about what happened that night. At least one person died; many more were injured. Buildings were blown to bits.

When the smoke cleared, and the chaos calmed, the town fathers were anxious to find out what had caused the explosion.

Was it an accident? Perhaps a careless smoker had tossed a warm match near the explosives arsenal; had the match started to smoulder, causing the explosion? Perhaps it was an act of God and an errant meteor or a flash of lightning had struck the building.

It wasn't until a farmer, strolling through his fields a few days after the explosion, discovered a strange-looking stone drilled a good 10 inches into the earth that investigators began piecing together what might have happened. Despite the force of the blast that had propelled the small rock into the ground, the stone was still covered with gunpowder, and a three-inch wick, which was secured to the stone by a lump of wax, was still attached. The suspicious find was turned over to investigators who, after a close examination, came to an inescapable conclusion. The blast wasn't caused by an act of God; someone had deliberately caused it. Originally, the wick of what was clearly an ignition device would have been considerably longer than what remained on the stone; whoever placed the device in the magazine and lit it would have had enough time to escape before the building, and everything around it, went up with a bang.

Now that investigators had discovered the how, they needed to answer the other obvious questions; who would cause such senseless damage and for what purpose? Could it have been the local drunk, Patrick Crockwell, up to a bit of no good and maybe a little angry at being tossed into the drunk tank once too often? Was the explosion caused by a bunch of kids who, after overhearing conversations about how the black powder could blast through miles of granite, wanted to see it in action for themselves? Or was it Honora Walsh, the Irish spinster who, earlier that day, had threatened a group of nasty neighbourhood boys who'd been giving her a hard time? These possibilities were soon discarded—they were petty problems, too small to warrant such a damaging response.

Investigators then asked another disturbing question: who had something to gain from blowing up the magazine? Even that question didn't give officials the boost they needed to find the killer. It wasn't until investigators asked who had access to the building that the name Alexander Keith Jr. came up. He was a long-time customer, knew how to schmooze just about anyone he met and had become fast friends with the fellow who ran the place. The magazine manager had been laid up in bed for six weeks before the explosion, and, according to one source, the attendant had given the arsenal key to Keith. Could it be that a member of one of the city's most prominent families was responsible for such complete, wholesale destruction?

Sandy found himself under the scrutiny of Halifax police, answering their probing questions. When was he last at the arsenal? What state was the building in? Who else might have had a key? Investigators faced the tough challenge of questioning the nephew of the prominent Alexander Keith Sr., three-time mayor and prominent businessman, without sounding accusatory. Alexander "the Younger" silenced investigators with his cool manner and well-thought-out answers. He wasn't the only person with access to the magazine, he testified; anyone who needed to get into the magazine just had to pick up the key at a neighbouring shop. Deflecting controversial testimony on the subject, the suspected bomber went on to say that the magazine was often very messy. Gunpowder often littered the floor—a potential fire hazard, if there ever was one—and Sandy himself had to get down on his hands and knees to clean it up. He even complained about the magazine keeper, saying that the man was difficult to get in touch with, and wasn't as reliable as he should be.

Frustrated by a lack of evidence, and reluctant to accuse a Keith of the crime outright, investigators promised a £500 (currency at the time was Canadian pounds sterling) reward to anyone who could shed light on the mystery. No one came forward. It seemed that Sandy could breathe a sigh of relief—almost. Although he was never found guilty of the crime in a court of law, one businessman who claimed he lost $50,000 because of the explosion wasn't going to let the incident go without being compensated for his loss. He was so certain that the cocky Sandy Keith was guilty that he demanded to be reimbursed. The businessman allegedly received his money, which amounted to a small fortune in those days, likely from the family coffers of Alexander Keith Sr.

Sandy must have thought highly of his namesake or, at least, played the part; after all, he'd forfeited a relationship with his own father in favour of building one with his powerful uncle. It was a well-deserved loyalty, especially in light of the situation that arose from the magazine explosion. Sandy's father could have never come up with the money required to pay the irate businessman, and, despite Sandy's suspected careless and greedy nature, family was still family. By now, Alexander Sr. was aware of several of his nephew's misdeeds. The elder Alexander even discovered that his nephew was thought to have taken on his uncle's identity, at times, and yet Alexander Sr. still kept his nephew in his employ.

Sandy wasn't without his complaints, however. He was envious of his uncle's success, both in business and within the social fabric of Halifax life. He was doubly envious of his cousin Donald, heir to the Keith fortunes. Sandy was also frustrated because, according to stories he later shared, his uncle was pressuring him to marry one of his spinster cousins. It became clear to the young man, now in his 30s, that he'd have to strike out on his own, become his own self-made man, and to keep up with his expensive tastes, he'd have to do it in style.

THE WAR YEARS

As Canada was being explored and conquered by small increments, its sovereignty being haggled over, the country's neighbours to the south were facing a power struggle of their own. In 1861, as Abraham Lincoln was being sworn in as the 16th president of the United States of America, 11 states—all located in the south—rebelled against the new president and his anti-slavery stance by seceding from the Union and forming the Confederate States of America, also known as the Confederacy. Such a treasonous act demanded an official response, and, before long, the American Civil War had become the focal point of the growing nation.

The war also affected Canada, especially harbour communities such as Halifax, which had ties to its southern neighbours. In fact, many Halifax residents outwardly sympathized with the Confederacy. However, Alexander Sr., now a member of the provincial government, threw in his loyalties with the Union. No doubt weighing which side would provide him with the most options, Sandy threw his hat in with the Confederacy, foreseeing an opportunity to profit from siding with the wealthy cotton farmers of the deep south, who would no doubt require transportation to export their crops and import the goods they'd become so accustomed to. In short, the war spelled adventure for the younger Keith as completely as it spelled opportunity.

By now, Alexander Jr. had moved from Keith Hall, his uncle's home, to one of his own. He'd also left his uncle's employ and was looking for ways to make his own way in the world. Already seemingly well-versed in deception, Sandy wasted no time in renting an office on Hollis Street and offering his services as a broker for several Southern concerns. He quickly learned the art of blockade-running, twisting it to give him even greater returns by making a sale and promising certain cargo but delivering something altogether different and, most importantly, less valuable.

A successful blockade-runner was a ship with power, speed and a first-rate crew that could manoeuvre around Union-blockaded seashores and deliver goods to Southern communities cut off from their regular suppliers. They promised much-yearned-for food items, such as coffee and liquor, as well as much-needed military supplies. Money was paid up front for the goods, and, although what was often shipped was little better than spoiled goods or worthless, second-hand freight, Southerners had no choice but to continue employing these methods of acquiring the provisions they needed and hope for the best. Their only other option was to do without.

The Southern states relied on the sale of cotton for their economic well-being; with Union blockades making transportation difficult, plantation farmers relied on blockade-runners to transport their bales of cotton, much of which was destined for British textile mills. It's little wonder that Sandy, and many other residents of Halifax, sided with the Confederacy—supplying the South provided a healthy economy for Halifax, which, as a major neutral port city, was fully equipped for the task of blockade-running. Sandy knew he had the cunning to make a pretty good living by taking advantage of the situation.

Although John Wilkinson, captain of the ship *Robert E. Lee*, once described Sandy as a "coarse, ill-bred vulgarian," there was little doubt that Sandy knew how to court his Southern guests while they were in Halifax. Champagne flowed as easily as the words of flattery and friendship with which Sandy cajoled his newfound friends. He knew he could go a long way by pouring on the honey and sparing the vinegar, and visiting Southerners lapped up his hospitality. Through his networking efforts, Sandy gained the trust of a large clientele, many of whom entrusted him with several thousands of dollars at a time and, in turn, expected him to acquire certain goods.

The more Sandy schmoozed with Southern visitors, the more he took on the role of a Southern gentleman himself. A turn of phrase here, a hand gesture there, a certain way of holding his head—he so clearly absorbed the mannerisms of his Southern clients that, if you didn't know from where the young man hailed, you might actually think he was new to Halifax. And because imitation is the greatest form of flattery, Keith's efforts garnered him increasing loyalty.

Ann Larabee, in her book *The Dynamite Fiend*, describes Keith this way: "Through flattery and indulgence, Keith became the man to know in Halifax for all Southerners with any business, and that included swaggering privateers and raiders who managed to entirely confuse their political cause with lust for profit. The idea, actively promoted by the Confederate government, was to do whatever damage possible to the property of a superior enemy, encouraging terrorist deeds with substantial rewards." Keith embraced this kind of philosophy; to his way of looking at things, it was almost a necessity if he was to make money.

And the more desperate the situation became for the Southern states, the more money its desperate residents handed over to Sandy Keith in their quest to obtain supplies.

In July 1864, Alexander Keith disguised himself as A.K. Thompson, an alias he'd embraced more and more fully as the years went by. As Thompson, Keith travelled from Halifax to Philadelphia, Pennsylvania. His mission was to purchase two steam engines for a man named Luther Smoot. The Southerner was anxious to acquire the locomotives and transport them to Virginia, where they'd run cotton along the Southern railroads, bringing the precious cargo to Southern seaports. Entrusted with $85,000 of his clients' money, Keith ordered the two engines from Norris Locomotive Works in Philadelphia. The engines had to be paid for in advance of their construction, and Keith willingly parted with $12,000 for each engine—$24,000 of the $25,000 Smoot invested in the deal. The reason Keith still had $60,000 in his possession was because he had sold those same two engines to two other clients—the Petersburg Steamship Company, which had given Keith $20,000 to presumably make the same deal, and a private investor named James Foreman, who'd given Sandy $40,000 for the engines.

On August 16, after being tipped off that the two engines ordered for Smoot were really destined for the Southern states and not Canada, which is where they were being shipped, Canadian officials inspected the completed engines and declared that their wheel measurements wouldn't work on Canadian rails, and the

Canadian government confiscated the engines. Keith had known this would happen; in fact, he'd planned for it. He was already prepared to deliver the news to each of his clients who, unaware of the others' existence and that they were victims of a lucrative scam, thought their money was lost because of the government confiscation.

When the loss was discovered, the Petersburg Steamship Company swallowed the loss. Foreman focused his fight to regain the $40,000 he invested in a legal battle with his partner, George Lang—though why he chose to do this isn't clear. The only one to doggedly pursue Keith, refusing to give up his $25,000 without a long, hard fight, was Luther Smoot. But that was a fight that Keith would deal with at a later time. At this point, now that he'd discovered how to swindle clients by promising goods, losing them in transit and pocketing the profits, he had a few more plans to hatch.

Keith was busy moving from one scam to another. He was hired by affluent Virginia transplants Georgina and Norman Walker to procure a $40,000 shipment of pork, a shipment that mysteriously went astray, the money lining Keith's pockets. And then there was the *Caledonia*, a ship titled to Keith by his friends, Charles and Gazaway Lamar—it was fairly common practice to list a British subject as the owner of a ship to avoid capture by Union Federal agents. Keith pocketed the insurance money for the ship, which conveniently sank just off the shores of Nova Scotia. The sinking enraged the real owner of the ship,

H.W. Kinsman of Charleston (now North Carolina), but he couldn't address the fraud through legal channels. He would have to even the score on his own terms.

It was some time before Keith, the always cheerful, presumably easygoing and charismatic businessman, was ever suspected of committing the cons he was eventually blamed for; it was a long time before anyone truly understood the lengths to which he'd go to pull them off. He stopped at nothing to make money; his appetite for fine cuisine, extravagant clothing and exceptional libations was not easily satiated and cost a lot of money to maintain. Even his closest friends, family members and business partners weren't exempt from his schemes if he could make money from them. Before Keith, using the alias A.K. Thompson, left Halifax on a dreary, late-December day in 1864, for Boston, Massachusetts, and later New York City, he had one more landmark scheme in mind.

This scheme wasn't restricted to the loss of capital—it would cost nothing less than the life of a friend and business partner.

To Con a Con Man

Keith's friend and fellow blockade-runner Patrick Martin wasn't the nicest man around. Like Keith, he wasn't averse to making a quick buck, even if it meant blurring the lines between what was completely above-board and what might be considered a little on the shady side. Keith, however, would take things further if it meant increasing his wealth. It didn't faze him that innocent people, or even someone he'd shared a laugh with over a glass of brandy, might get hurt in the process. To make money on his latest and most brazen scheme, Keith allegedly planned for Martin's demise.

The Civil War was near its end; recognizing that the Confederates he supported were not only losing the war but also were running out of money, Martin planned to leave the risky business of blockade-running with a blast, earning himself a nice little chunk of change in the process. After being approached by John Wilkes Booth, the Shakespearean actor who would eventually be hanged for assassinating President Lincoln, Martin agreed to provide Booth with letters of intro-duction and the financial means to kidnap the president and hold him hostage in exchange for the release of Confederate prisoners of war. Martin also agreed to transport the actor's extensive and costly wardrobe from Montréal, where Booth had been working, to his destination of Baltimore, Maryland. The wardrobe, which Booth had insured for at least $25,000, was being shipped on one of Martin's last blockade-runners.

As Martin's business partner and close friend, Keith infused the plot with a few ideas of his own. He purchased a hefty insurance policy on Martin's ships and cargo and, with Martin's blessing, Keith was entrusted with both papers and power of attorney, should Martin meet with an untimely death. Then, playing up Martin's thirst for adventure, Keith suggested

Martin outfit a less-than-seaworthy vessel and oversee the safe passage of this last, valuable shipment. Against the wishes of his wife and daughter, and against all good common sense—blockade-running was dangerous at the best of times, more so on treacherous November seas—Martin boarded what was possibly his most unsound ship. Having enjoyed a few glasses of ale the night before with a group of British officers, Martin boarded the ship and slept there for the night. By morning, the schooner was gone.

It was Martin's last voyage. Shortly after leaving Halifax, both of Martin's schooners perished in the stormy waters. Although some of the crewmembers safely made it to shore, the entire cargo was lost, as was Martin. He was never seen nor heard from again. Mother Nature had taken its course, and Keith's gamble paid off.

Keith didn't bat an eye. Shortly after hearing the news, he calmly visited the insurance agent and collected roughly $100,000 for his loss, with no thought whatsoever to his friend's demise. Martin's wife and children were the reasonable recipients of the money, but it was Keith's name on the papers, and, in the eyes of the law, the money belonged to him. In the eyes of friendship or morality or goodness, the money ought to have been shared with Martin's family. But, no. Keith's only concern was for his own well-being. Although Martin's family was left penniless, Keith's main concern was planning his next move and looking ahead to a life of leisure. And though there might have been some speculation that Keith had arranged for Martin's ship to sink, as most who knew Keith concurred, he wouldn't leave his financial future to chance or "an act of God." But there was never any concrete evidence that he planted a bomb or tampered in any way with the seaworthiness of Martin's ship. At most, Keith could be seen as a heartless and greedy man.

By now, some of Keith's acquaintances weren't just talking about the possibility that Keith might have sunk his friend's ship to collect the insurance money, they were starting to examine Keith's business transactions and question their legitimacy. The Walkers, for example, were still looking for their pork or, in lieu of the goods, some sort of compensation for their loss. Luther Smoot wanted his steam engines. And Keith was becoming increasingly aware of the fact that because he'd swindled so many people, it wouldn't be long before someone caught up with him and demanded their pound of flesh. So Keith planned his last Halifax con—he arranged to disappear.

It was the end of December 1864. Under the guise of reclaiming the wayward pork for the Walkers, Keith spent a last night of revelry in Halifax, toasting his friends and wishing them a Happy New Year and broadcasting to anyone who'd listen that he was headed for Boston. Disguising himself as an entrepreneur travelling on business, Keith again took the alias A.K. Thompson—the alias he would permanently acquire—and travelled to Boston, where the pork shipment was supposedly being stored. While Keith was waiting for the arrival from Halifax of his lady love, Mary Clifton, who Keith had elevated from the lowly position of hotel chambermaid to kept woman, he was busy orchestrating another swindle. He forged a bill for a shipment of cotton from Boston to Scotland, charging $5000 more than its actual cost and keeping the difference. Petty cash to a man who'd just made a $100,000 haul, but the thrill of the chase was reason enough to pull off one more fraud.

With Mary safely arrived in Boston, Keith was on the move again. This time, the scammer and his mistress were headed for New York and the Manhattan high life. While the couple was dining on succulent steaks and downing flutes of champagne, the men Keith had swindled back in Halifax and elsewhere in the New World were beginning to recognize they'd been had. Keith was smart to flee—estimates of Keith's scams ranged somewhere from $150,000 to $300,000, amounts equivalent to millions of dollars in today's terms. Understandably, he was constantly looking over his shoulder in fear for his life. Eventually, Keith's nerves got the best of him; he wasn't just worried anymore, he was physically ill. Poor Mary waited on him hand and foot, tending to his every need and helping him recover from the bodily manifestation of his mental anguish.

But Keith's loyalty to the young woman who'd given up everything to follow her lover across a stormy ocean and into a foreign, sometimes unfriendly, land was as good as his word—which wasn't very good at all. As soon as Keith learned that his apprehension was justified, he made travel plans. A man named Robert Grissom would apparently stop at nothing to find the man he'd entrusted with $4000 worth of gold coins in Halifax and who, instead of delivering them safely, had apparently lost them at sea. Pulling double duty, Grissom was also tracking Keith down for the Walkers, who were still on the hunt for their pork. Frightened, Keith told Mary that he had to leave town but would send for her as soon as he was settled. Of course, Keith didn't see fit to leaving poor Mary with two coins to rub together; while she waited, she had to fend for herself, eventually taking work, once again, as a hotel chambermaid. It took her some time to realize that her ticket out of the impoverished life she had been living was gone. Keith had left her penniless and far from home. By then, she'd also discovered she was pregnant with Keith's twins.

Meanwhile, in January 1865, Keith arrived in St. Louis, settling in at the Southern Hotel and gaining a feel for the political climate of Missouri. Although he told Mary he'd send for her, he never did. Instead, he hooked up with an old friend he'd nicknamed "The Frenchman" and masqueraded as the Frenchman's cousin, basing the farce on the fact that both men shared the same last name of Thompson. He soon blended into the Missouri landscape and a whole new life.

THE BEGINNING OF THE END

In the spring of 1865, Keith and his "cousin," the Frenchman, headed across Missouri to the remote, German-speaking community of Highland, Illinois, where the Frenchman had family. Highland was a long way from major transportation routes, and its reputation as a tight-knit community would preclude, in Keith's mind, any of his enemies from thinking he'd be living there. After all, Keith liked to be noticed and was used to living the high life. Opportunities for that kind of lifestyle weren't plentiful in Highland. And, although Keith was adept at blending in with almost any crowd, his German was atrocious. With such poor command of the language, he wasn't likely to convince anyone of his claim to be his Parisian cousin's long-lost German relative. Still, Keith was pretty sure he could pour on the charm and weave his way into Highland's high society, such as it was. Surprisingly, he was remarkably successful at it.

As Mary was recognizing that she, too, had been conned by the master con artist and was making plans to return to Halifax, Keith was wheedling his way into the lives of Highlanders. One young lass in particular caught his eye and, should he have had any lingering yearnings for Mary, they quickly dissipated the moment he saw Cecelia Paris. The daughter of a prominent St. Louis milliner, Cecelia loved the lifestyle of the wealthy—they were the only ones who could afford the kind of hats Cecelia and her mother made. Cecelia wanted that lifestyle. She wanted to rub shoulders with the rich and powerful, with women of taste and substance and men of high standing, on more levels than during the purchase of their newest hat. In essence, her aspirations were similar to Keith's. The two connected—they were soul mates of a co-dependent variety. Cecelia was far more refined than the rough-around-the-edges, and sometimes outright vulgar, Keith, and she provided her new lover with a chance to elevate himself. Keith had money when he met Cecelia and could afford to offer her adventure and a lavish lifestyle by mingling in the kind of social circles she longed to move in.

Theirs was a whirlwind romance: elaborate dinners, walks in the moonlight and long talks, all accompanied by endlessly fluttering stomachs. The couple never tired of each other when they were together, and they spent the time they were apart pining for the other. A few months after she met Keith, Cecelia recognized there was still much about the mysterious man that she didn't know; nevertheless, by the end of the summer, they were married. A deeper understanding of some of her new husband's behaviours she'd garner through observation; others remained unsettlingly obscure. He was prone to odd "business" trips and would leave for periods of time with little or no explanation. Sometimes, he appeared nervous for no apparent reason, and his sleep was frequently disrupted by ongoing nightmares. Then suddenly, he disappeared, swept away in the middle of a cold December night after a Christmas party by his old nemesis, Luther Smoot. More than a year had passed since Smoot had been swindled of $25,000 by Keith. Accompanied by U.S. Marshal David Phillips and St. Louis detective John Egan, Smoot confronted Keith and demanded his money. Arrest warrant in hand, Phillips ordered Keith to accompany them back to St. Louis and to either cough up the money he owed or pay the penalty through the courts.

As persistent as Smoot was in interrogating Keith and demanding his money back, Keith was just as unrelenting in his denial that he had any money at all. Even when Smoot brought in the big guns, in the person of General William Tecumseh Sherman, Keith didn't back down. He was broke; he swore to the fact. Keith's armour never cracked. Sherman was inclined to encourage Smoot to let sleeping dogs lie, but Smoot was dogged in his persistence. In the end, Keith relented somewhat—he was anxious to get home to his wife—and confessed to having $19,500 in bonds and savings but nothing more. The men agreed that Keith would pay Smoot $10,000—less than half the money Keith had swindled from the man, but it was something, nonetheless.

After a 10-day absence from his new wife, Keith was back in Cecelia's arms, drowning her with words of comfort and begging her forgiveness, then bombarding her with stories of the bad men who'd unjustly hunted him down and commanded him to pay them money. They had to move, Keith told her. Far away. So far away that none of the bad men would ever track him down again. On January 13, 1866, the newlyweds boarded the steamer *Hermann* and set sail for Germany, arriving in Bremerhaven 12 days later.

With about $45,000 in their pockets, Keith and Cecelia found suitable accommodations and slipped their way into high society, dining and drinking with other wealthy Americans who, like them, were seeking an exotic life in Europe. With a new identity firmly established, altering his original alias slightly to William King Thompson, Keith and Cecelia toured the European continent, enjoying the high life without a thought to an ongoing plan for their financial security.

Cecelia apparently wasn't aware of how her husband provided for her, and she didn't really care to know. It only mattered that she was maintained in the lifestyle she'd become accustomed to and so dearly admired, and, for a time, it seemed that her loving William was quite adept at doing just that. In time, the couple welcomed one, then another, baby, until in the end they had four children, three girls and a boy. But the good days were quickly coming to an end. The well was running dry. By 1871, Keith's $45,000 had dwindled to less than $5000 and, within a year, to half that. Other than an occasional supply of money, which Keith, while out on unexplained "business excursions," would ship to Cecelia in bankers' drafts, the family had no reliable source of income. If they continued spending money so freely, and neither Keith nor Cecelia seemed inclined to stop, Keith would have to make some concrete plans for his family's financial future. If he didn't, they'd be ousted from their comfortable, albeit increasingly humble, living arrangements and sleeping on the streets.

But Keith had a plan. Combining his experience in blowing up the Halifax magazine and his familiarity with cashing insurance policies on bogus goods later destroyed in catastrophic shipwrecks, William devised what he believed was a foolproof get-rich-quick scheme: he would insure a load of goods for considerably more than its worth and then, using an explosive, such as the newly invented dynamite, blow up the ship.

What Keith needed to pull off his plan was help. He approached several prestigious clockmakers, looking for someone who could construct a spring-loaded timepiece: he needed it to set his bomb to explode at a preordained time. While he had one, then another, clockmaker working on the device he'd created in his imagination, Keith went in search of the second necessary component to his plan—dynamite. In 1867, the noted chemist Alfred Nobel had developed and patented his deadly combination of stabilized nitroglycerine and diatomaceous earth. The resulting dynamite was a compact explosive that was relatively light and easy to transport and could cause great amounts of damage with a single flicker of a flame. Despite its dangerous nature, dynamite was surprisingly easy to acquire, because restrictions on its use were yet to be developed. Nonetheless, Keith was still careful about where, how and how much dynamite he purchased—he didn't want to draw any unnecessary attention.

To avoid detection by the authorities, should his planned disaster blow up in his face, Keith took on the persona of Russian businessman Teadro Wiskoff and later as W.J. Garcie of Jamaica when he was out doing business. As the Russian Wiskoff, Keith told Ignas Rhind, one of the clockmakers he'd contracted, that he was looking for a mechanism to effectively cut silk threads at his silk factory. Keith had approached J.J. Fuchs of Bernburg to tackle the project in the spring of 1873, asking him to build him a silent 10-day clock, but the intensely inquisitive clockmaker had asked too many questions, and Keith had shied away. The decision to hire someone else was disappointing—Fuchs had such a sound reputation for constructing long-running timepieces—but Rhind was also thought of highly, and Keith believed he'd get the job done.

Rhind also had a reputation, having already created a workable eight-day clock. Keith upped the ante, asking him to create a 12-day clock with a powerful hammer that would snap with tremendous force once the clock had wound down. The challenge itself was so intriguing that Rhind was more interested in the problem than questioning Keith about his use for such a device. It wasn't long before Rhind generated a blueprint for the mechanism, but it took his technician, Carl Gluckshall, five long months to construct it. Anxious to put his plan to work and getting increasingly desperate for cash, Keith was frustrated by the amount of time it was taking Rhind and his partner to complete the project. He was even angrier when it didn't work the way he wanted it to—Keith needed the force to be strong enough to detonate a large amount of dynamite if his plan to sink a ship had any hope of success. As it was, the mechanism simply couldn't do the job.

By this time, Keith had spent a lot of money paying Rhind, buying dynamite, travelling between destinations and approaching companies to buy insurance on a barrel of "valuable goods" he wanted to transport. Instead of putting his plan into action, Keith was faced with spending even more money to get Rhind's mechanism improved and arguing with insurance agents, who were becoming wiser in the ways of the world and less inclined to insure things they hadn't inventoried. In March 1875, two years after first approaching Fuchs, Keith was once again talking to the clockmaker, this time, asking him to make the changes he felt were necessary to Rhind's mechanism. Buying Keith's businessman persona much better this time round, Fuchs went to work and created a stronger and silent device. Keith was so thrilled, he paid the man an extra $25.

He wasn't quite as thrilled when he did a trial run, shipping a barrel containing the explosive dynamite and the clockwork required to detonate it on the *Rhein*, which was sailing from Germany to New York, only to have the ship arrive safely in port. Operating under the alias George S. Thomas, Keith collected his cargo and made plans for his next attempt.

In September, Keith withdrew the last of his cash from the bank and bounced a cheque. While creditors were looking for Keith to make good, Keith was busy talking another bank into giving him a line of credit. He needed the cash if he was to finally pull off this last con. By December, Keith knew he was facing a do-or-die situation.

Keith insured a barrel he told insurance agents was full of caviar, for a mere £150 (the equivalent of about $270 in today's currency). The barrel was to be placed in the cargo hold of the *Mosel*, set to depart from Bremen on December 11. The ship was sailing to New York but would stop in Southampton to pick up the survivors of the *Deutschland*, which was shipwrecked along the sandbars near the Thames Estuary and the North Sea. Keith would be on board for a time but planned to get off at the scheduled Southampton stop. By the time the *Mosel* met with its tragic demise, the man who'd eventually be labelled by authorities as "The Dynamite Fiend" would be on his way home for Christmas holidays. And the entire scheme, the destruction to property and human carnage it would cause, would net the con man £150, not even enough to clear some of his immediate debt.

The air was crisp on December 11. Passengers loitering on the docks and wrapping their coats a little closer around them welcomed the final boarding call blaring from the *Mosel* and scrambled up the ramp. They said their final farewells to the loved ones they were leaving behind, while the last pieces of luggage were being lifted into the cargo hold. Keith made his way toward his first-class cabin, chatting with his fellow travellers along the way and glancing, every once in a while, across the ship's deck and over the open water that lay before him. Shortly after he arrived at his cabin, while attempting to organize his surroundings and plan for his short voyage, Keith was thrown to the floor with the sudden rocking of the ship. Intense heat and a blast of hot air filtered into the hallways, and someone suggested that perhaps there had been an explosion in the ship's boiler room. But Keith could guess at what had really happened.

Rushing back to the upper deck to survey the damage, Keith was appalled by his own murderous deed. Burned and mangled bodies lay everywhere, like a carpet of blood, flesh and bone. Shards of burning wood and twisted metal replaced the previously tranquil setting on the wharf. The devastation was catastrophic but much less so than it would have been had the explosion occurred when the ship was crossing the Atlantic. The New York Times reported that if the explosion had taken place at sea, the entire ship would have been destroyed, and it was quite possible that no one would have ever known what had happened.

Had the disaster occurred at sea, Keith would have cashed in his meagre insurance policy, without anyone being the wiser. Adept at compartmentalizing his actions, beliefs, feelings and behaviours, Keith would have walked away with little, if any, remorse for his actions. Instead, he found himself faced with the harsh outcome of his scheme. One can only imagine the emotions flooding him. Was he angry that his plans had not succeeded? Or was he sorry that he'd ever committed something so unspeakable and was disgusted by his own avarice? Regardless of his feelings, it's a safe bet he was desperate for a way out.

Meanwhile, emergency personnel were trying to help the wounded and dying. Fires were extinguished, and officers tried to discover if another explosion was imminent. Once the situation was brought under control, investigators pieced together what they believed caused the explosion. It wasn't a malfunctioning boiler. It appeared that workers were trying to move some kind of barrel containing explosives onto the cargo hold of the ship. Immediately, questions arose about what kind of explosives were involved and where they had come from. Were these explosives placed there for malicious reasons, or was the barrel legitimate cargo that accidentally went off? These were all questions that investigators needed to answer. As it happened, Keith sped up the investigation considerably by immediately throwing suspicion on himself.

With the loss of the gangway, Keith lost his only means of escape. Frantically, he demanded that the captain get him to shore but was told it was impossible. Trapped and panicking, like a wild animal in a small metal cage, Keith retreated to his cabin. It's impossible to know if it was remorse or if he was simply overcome by his latest failure and the realization that he'd never collect the meagre insurance money that motivated his next move. Either way, he came to a decision about his future. It was a decision that wouldn't allow for any second thoughts and was about as self-serving as every other decision he'd ever made.

Keith started writing. He first penned a note to Cecilia, telling of his love for her and the children and saying goodbye. He then scrawled a message to the captain of the *Mosel*, dated December 11, 1875:

Please send this money you will find in my pocket—
20 pounds sterling
80 marks German money
My wife resides at
14 Residenze Strasse
Strehlen
By Dresden
What I have seen today
I cannot stand.
W.K. Thomas

Having completed this last task, Keith sat on his couch and pulled the trigger on his revolver. Twice.

Two bullets to the head would, for most people, mean certain death. Not so for Keith. One of the bullets went through his cheek and settled behind his right eye, paralyzing the left side of his body. Rescuers found him writhing in pain, moaning in agony but not dead. It would be several days before he finally succumbed, and, during that time, he was interrogated by the police, investigators and his wife. What happened? How was he involved? Why would he want to blow up the ship? Were others involved in the plot? Were there other bombs targeting other ships? Keith remained tight-lipped, reiterating stories of his years as a Civil War blockade-runner and his time in the U.S., knitting together a blend of fact and fiction so convincingly that he perhaps believed his own lies.

He never revealed his childhood in Scotland nor his youth in Canada.

Many months passed before the investigation into the Bremerhaven catastrophe, also known as the Thompson disaster, came to a reasonable conclusion. News agencies in Europe wired the U.S. with reports on the tragedy as news came in, reluctant to wait for more thorough, accurate and detailed explanations of what had happened. For a while, Keith was known as either William Henry or William King, with the surname of Thompson, Thomassen or Thomas. Various news stories listed him as having been born in Brockholt, Prussia, in Westphalia, Germany, in Brooklyn or New York or as being Swabian by birth and emigrating to the U.S. at age two or sometime thereafter.

It wasn't until Cecilia arrived that Keith was formally identified as William King Thompson, the only name to which she would admit to knowing her husband, though, in one of her correspondences, she did slip and call him Alexander. Even under constant interrogation by investigators, Cecilia refused to admit to knowing anything of her husband's business—though, if she did suspect he was into something, she gave no indication that she went out of her way to find out what that "something" was. In the end, officials declared Cecilia innocent of her husband's wrongdoings and allowed her, after visiting him, to go on her way. Cecilia returned to her family in the U.S. and lived in relative obscurity.

The further unravelling of Keith's true identity took many months and involved the efforts of the world-famous Pinkerton Agency, based at the time in Chicago. In the end, the personas Keith had adopted were stripped away, and the man the world had known under so many aliases was identified as Alexander Keith Jr. of Halifax, Nova Scotia: brewmaster's nephew, blockade-runner and alleged cold-hearted con artist.

HISTORY REVISITED

Bremerhaven tourists aren't likely to find anyone who remembers the story of what, at one point, was known as the "Thomas Catastrophe." It's unclear if Keith's wax bust is on display at any Berlin museum, and the original wax museum no longer exists. But if the bust were still around, patrons would need to read the fine print to know the name of the person represented and to understand the evil perpetrated by the "Dynamite Fiend" during his lifetime.

As to the Dynamite Fiend's decapitated head...sometime after Soldan's examination, Keith's head found its way to the "museum of crime, Police House Bremen," where, over the next several decades, it reminded residents of a horrible time in their city's history. But if you're visiting Bremen, and have a macabre enough temperament to want to view the exhibit, you will be sadly disappointed. The specimen of Keith's head in a jar no longer exists. According to one source, in a bizarre case of serendipity, Keith's head was blown up in World War II, when Allied bombs hit Bremen harbour in 1944. The story goes that Keith's head was among the other human carnage resulting from the bomb, and the unidentified bits and pieces of human victims were buried together in a mass grave.

Chapter Eight

Turning Over a New Leaf
NICK LYSYK

⁓

It's the big bad bank against me.

—Nick Lysyk, shortly after being charged with fraud, commenting on the fact that the bank he was accused of defrauding
had withheld his final paycheque, holiday pay and severance

EVERYDAY EDMONTON

He was just an ordinary guy, with an in-at-nine,
home-at-five, white-collar job. Decent pay. Pretty
wife. A daughter who was the apple of his eye.
Nice house. Not a bad portfolio, really. The small-town guy
from Mundare, Alberta, moves to the big city, makes good and
lands himself a management job at the Wolf Willow Place branch
of the Bank of Montreal, located in Edmonton's west end. Now,
at 50-something, he should be able to ease up a little.

But he had a problem. He was a tad flat. He was that
nice, predicable fellow who walked to the streetlights to cross
the road, rather than jaywalk. Some of the people he knew went
so far as to call him boring. A "typical nerd," even.

And the way people looked down on him couldn't help but deflate any small bit of self-esteem he might have salvaged. If only he had money. Lots of money.

Maybe he'd buy a car. A flashy new car. Red maybe. He'd always wanted a Corvette, a dream from his younger days. A red Corvette would be a good choice. But a Mercedes, well, a Mercedes would spell class and smell like money.

Maybe he'd buy them both. Hell, he'd even get himself a classic car or two, maybe a Jeep for trips to the lake and a BMW for added clout.

Then he'd ditch the wife.

A younger woman would be good for his image.

BACK AT THE BANK

Nicholas Andrew Lysyk had been in banking since the 1970s. After three decades in banking, and several years as the manager of the Bank of Montreal, he knew his job. He was responsible for the day-to-day operations of his bank: for overseeing his staff, for communicating with other branches and corporate head office, for accounting procedures and for customer lending and account maintenance, just to name a few.

He also knew about the kinds of things that raised suspicions and what went unnoticed. It was all about the numbers—and he was good at numbers.

It started with a single bogus loan. Lysyk set it up on December 6, 1996. He was probably tired of being the predictable, dependable, good guy you could set your clock by. He was tired of being taken for granted, tired of being the "nerd." Christmas was coming, and he was going to show everyone that he knew how to have a good time. This year, he wouldn't be boring. This year, he'd be inventive, extravagant, even. This year he'd be St. Nicholas.

No doubt, a man with no previous criminal experience would have been nervous. Sure, he might have had a good time spending the money from that first loan, but it's conceivable that he was looking over his shoulder for a very long time. But, when no one noticed, when red flags didn't go up weeks and months down the road, Lysyk's confidence skyrocketed to such an extent that he decided to try it again. After all, he had friends to think about. A family to spoil. Another small loan would give him a bit of freedom, a little leeway to buy the guys a drink after work. It would help him loosen up.

By August 2, 2002, Lysyk had found a total of 64 excuses to issue fraudulent loans to, for the most part, nonexistent people, and in the process pocket an estimated $16,335,000. (It is important to note that two of the loans were repaid the day they were granted, which makes a person wonder whether Lysyk did feel guilty, or if he was concerned he was becoming too obvious. The 62 remaining loans totalled $15,970,000.)

Then, one day, he wasn't the cool guy anymore.

Now, he was the subject of water-cooler talk across the entire city of Edmonton. And he wasn't being talked about in a good way.

The Facts

Nick Lysyk had been in banking for as long as his wife, Jennifer Busdegan, knew him. The two met when Jennifer was just 15 and Nick was 19. Four years later, they married. By that time in his career, Lysyk was well established at the Toronto Dominion Bank, where he worked before moving on to the Bank of Montreal in 1990.

As a bank manager, Lysyk was pulling in about $60,000 a year—enough to live on but not an extravagant wage, by any means. When he started spending large amounts of money, one would think his wife or daughter or even a friend would have asked him if he'd won the lottery and forgotten to mention it to anyone. But they didn't have to—at least, not at first. Two of Lysyk's family members had passed away, one in 1999 and another in 2001. Each left a significant inheritance. The estate of one family member totalled $1,151,622.32. Although Lysyk only collected a third of that inheritance, it was still a significant boost to his annual income. It was certainly enough money to live a little high on the hog for a while.

But Lysyk's inheritance didn't explain the ongoing spending spree. From 1996 until he was discovered in 2002, money seemed to flow through Lysyk's hands like water, and yet no one appeared to publicly question him about it.

Lysyk's bubble burst in August 2002, when he was finally arrested and charged. The public first learned about the middle-income bank manager who made off with record amounts of cash on August 14. It was a typical, but random, bank audit that raised questions about some irregularities. The questions began on August 6, when the auditor assigned to the bank noticed that Nick Lysyk's signature was remarkably similar to the signature of a woman who'd received a $220,000 loan. According to the loan documents, the woman used her GICs as collateral, but when the auditor checked them, those GICs were found to be nonexistent. One small inconsistency led to the discovery of another, until all the numbers started screaming that something was very wrong. They also added up to only one possible perpetrator—the loyal, long-suffering, straight as an arrow, sometimes nerdy bank manager who had approved the loans.

At first, Lysyk cried foul. He denied any complicity in the missing $16 million, which has been named one of the largest bank frauds in Canadian history. He thought the authorities were trying to make an example of him and argued that his employer had turned its back on him—he wasn't even given his last pay-cheque, nor was he handed his holiday and severance pay after he was let go. In Lysyk's mind, that was a little like saying he was guilty of the charges before he'd had his day in court.

Once the authorities were onto him, piecing together the sequence of activities over the previous six years pointed to a pretty straightforward scam.

"This was not a particularly elaborate scheme," Detective Richard Kracher, acting manager of the Edmonton Police Department's economic-crimes section told Jill Mahoney of the *Globe and Mail* in August 2002. "The record will show that this was a very, very simple thing, and you know it's the old adage—sometimes your best plans are your most simple ones."

On August 30, 2004, Lysyk realized that there was no way to escape a guilty conviction and pleaded guilty to fraud.

HOW VERY SAD

But what had Lysyk done with all that money? According to court documents, Lysyk spent a lot, $4.3 million of it, on himself. He bought those flashy cars he wanted—according to an *Edmonton Sun* story, he was the "registered owner of seven high-value vehicles." He got the flashy women, too, but they cost him.

Analysts who took inventory of the items and real estate that Lysyk had purchased identified 17 houses, condos or rental properties, 40 vehicles and about $3.58 million worth of credit card purchases. From what investigators could discover, Lillian Green, Lysyk's one-time girlfriend and escort, received the equivalent of $3.5 million in cash and merchandise. Lysyk also spread about $1.5 million among his family and friends and spent another $2.3 million spoiling eight female escorts during his six-year scam—he told police he was forced to do this because the women's associates were threatening him. He was pretty good to his ex-wife, too; she wound up with about $1 million, but by 2002 the couple had divorced.

On September 10, 2004, Lysyk was sentenced to seven years and four months in jail. He served nowhere near that time. Just 14 months later, he was out on day parole, and, in two and a half years, on February 19, 2007, he was granted full parole.

In its report, the parole board expressed some concerns about Lysyk. The report described Lysyk's "extreme greed and abuse of power," and that, given the right set of circumstances, "emotional turmoil, low self-esteem and a desire to be in seen in a positive fashion are stress factors that could cause [him] to return to fraudulent activity." To appropriately monitor Lysyk's activity, the parole board mandated that he report all his financial transactions to his parole officer until January 9, 2012, when his sentence expires.

Although a public auction of much of Lysyk's estate was held—the money raised was used to pay back some of the money he'd scammed—the bank is still out a lot of cash. Chances are Lysyk will be looking over his shoulder for the rest of his life.

WHY DID HE DO IT?

Some might believe the prime motivator that catapulted Lysyk's life from ordinary into the realm of bizarre was his low self-esteem; he wanted to be popular. Perhaps that was part of the issue, but according to Calgary forensic psychologist Dr. Marc Nesca, who spoke with the *Edmonton Sun* two days after Lysyk's guilty plea, Lysyk's problems were more complicated than that. Nesca suggested that Lysyk caught his wife with her boyfriend, and this might have put the banker into an "emotionally compromised state." It was the catalyst that propelled Lysyk to seek the comfort of a prostitute, and it might have been at least partly the reason for Lysyk's Jekyll and Hyde impersonation, shocking everyone who knew him.

Either way, Lysyk's criminal activities didn't make life better for him in the long run. As the old adage goes, "Crime doesn't pay."

It never does.

Chapter Nine

The Kind-Hearted Con Man

FERDINAND WALDO DEMARA

~

He may be six kinds of a liar,
He may be ten kinds of a fool,
He may be a wicked high flyer,
Beyond any reason or rule.
There may be a shadow above him,
Of ruin and woes to impend.
And I may not respect, but I love him,
Because—well because he's my friend...

–part of a verse penned to Ferdinand Waldo Demara
by one of his old shipmates on board the *Cayuga*
after news the authorities were looking for him

LAUNCHED

This was it, the adventure of a lifetime. Standing on the bridge of the HMCS *Cayuga* R04/218, the young man brushed the saltwater spray from his face as the ship rolled with the ebb and swell of the waves.

This wasn't just any sea voyage. This wasn't just any ship. The slightly rotund man with the endearing smile and jolly laugh was aboard a Tribal class destroyer, one of the Royal Canadian Navy's newest power ships. This streamlined vessel could not only could slice through the waters faster than most of its predecessors, but it was also equipped with more guns than any of the country's earlier destroyers.

The ship on which 29-year-old Ferdinand Waldo Demara was sailing on this brisk June day in 1951 was built at the Halifax Shipyards in Halifax, Nova Scotia. First launched on July 28, 1947, it was commissioned on October 20, 1947. The HMCS *Cayuga* was still a babe in the waters. Built to serve on Canada's Pacific coast, the ship was outfitted with a crew, sailed along the Atlantic coast and spent a time serving in Bermuda, before heading for its final destination of Esquimalt, British Columbia. Now, the *Cayuga,* carrying a dozen officers and almost 200 enlisted men, was leaving the Esquimalt harbour to serve in the Korean War.

The young doctor standing on the decks of the *Cayuga,* looking in the direction of the Korean Peninsula, the man everyone knew as Dr. Joseph C. Cyr, had one of the most prestigious jobs on board. It was also one of the most prestigious jobs of his career as a con man. Just a couple of days into his new assignment, he'd already conducted minor surgery on none other than his commanding officer.

Commander James Plomer was so busy preparing his ship and crew for sail that he hadn't taken the time to see a dentist regarding a tooth that was causing him mind-numbing pain. When Demara came on board, Plomer cornered his new surgeon-lieutenant and almost begged the man to remove the tooth immediately. Demara talked the commander into waiting until the morning. Of course, Demara had no knowledge whatsoever about dentistry, and so he locked himself in his private quarters and began to study up on the subject.

It was amazing what a large dose of Novocain could do to combat pain. All Demara had to do was inject the miracle drug into his commander's jaw, clamp his tooth extractor around the tooth and pop it out. It was remarkably simple, really, Demara thought. And the success of that first solo surgery boosted his confidence.

Of course, Demara knew he had lots to learn. He recognized that the challenging medical cases his assistant, known as the sick berth attendant, was anxious to work on would require significantly more skill than was needed for a simple tooth extraction. Still, he savoured the moment. It was moments just like this, when he was unexpectedly thrust into situations of intense pressure and expected to perform, that, instead of crumbling, like most people would, he managed to pull it all off. Which was exactly why he was doing this, wasn't it?

THE YOUNG YEARS

Ferdinand Waldo Demara first presented himself to the world in Lawrence, Massachusetts, just before Christmas in 1921, by all accounts a much-loved, only child of his New England–born mother and French Canadian father of the same name. Although he was a precocious child and a voracious reader, surprisingly, Ferdinand Jr. didn't stand out among his peers academically. His school grades were average; later in life he'd attribute his lack of a high-school diploma to being bored and sufficiently capable of learning everything he needed to know under his own tutelage. But, in reality, young Ferdinand was anything but average. In 1951, when Ferdinand bid farewell to the Canadian Navy after having pulled off the caper of a lifetime, his father told newspaper reporters that, as a boy, his son "was bright to the point of genius. Things came easily to him and he read constantly. There was nothing bad in him. He always wanted to help others—especially those who were suffering."

The problem was that Ferdinand didn't have a lot of patience as a child, and he didn't develop patience as an adult. He didn't have it in him to go through the necessary steps to gain an education for a particular career path. He was the kind of guy who liked to jump into things.

He also had a tough time accepting the more difficult parts of life. It deeply affected Ferdinand when his father, a successful man who'd gained considerable personal wealth through his co-ownership of several theatres in Lawrence, lost his businesses and the family's stately home and had to release the family's servants. The young Ferdinand's life devolved from that of a spoiled, wealthy, only child to a more ordinary existence, and he had a difficult time adjusting. He couldn't understand why the family's change in circumstances was beyond his father's control. He earnestly believed there was no such thing as having to settle for less, and, if you want something badly enough, you should be able to achieve it. The only two options in life were to do or not do. There was no such thing as "can't." It was a mantra Ferdinand applied to his own life, and, for the most part, he managed to get whatever he wanted.

Ferdinand started along his path to self-actualization by leaving school at the age of 15 and heading to a Trappist monastery in Valley Falls, Rhode Island. His desire for a cleric's life was a theme that followed him throughout the next five decades. Although his initial foray into monastic life only lasted two years, he eventually became a novice with the Brothers of Charity, based in Boston, and spent some time in Montréal washing dishes in a retreat for struggling clergy. Later in life, he returned to his desire for work in spiritual ministry. But there were a lot of intervening years during which he tried his hand at just about every line of work, weaving in and out of people's lives in the process.

"I don't want no more of army life..."

The first acquisition on his long list of alter egos was Anthony Ingolia. Having joined the U.S. Army and recognizing it was not for him, Demara stole Ingolia's personal papers in 1941.

In Demara's biography, *The Great Impostor,* author Robert Crichton explained that Demara believed motive was the main concern in whatever someone chose to do in life. As long as his motives were good, his actions couldn't be faulted.

> *Since his aim was to do good, anything he did to do it was always justified. With Demara, the end always justified the means. Stealing Ingolia's papers was not in itself a bad act if he didn't do bad things with them. Demara has always been blessed with a very personal conception of God looking down, reading the motives in his head and nodding approvingly. With that picture in his mind, he knew little shame and less fear.*

And so it was that Demara went AWOL from the army and, equipped with a new identity, booked into what's now known as the Abbey of Gethsemane, a Trappist monastery about 50 miles, or 80.5 kilometres, south of Louisville, Kentucky.

It wasn't long before the army was on to him, so Demara left the monastery and joined the navy. It was his first taste of the salty sea air and his first foray into the world of medicine. He applied for the navy's hospital school under a new false identity, Dr. Robert Linton French, a psychology professor fresh from a research fellowship at Yale University. He'd gathered all the personal data on French from a college catalogue; French had once served on the college faculty. Demara apparently didn't stay long in his new position and returned to the Gethsemane monastery. Struggling with the vows of silence, Demara refocused his attentions in another order, where vows of silence were not a prerequisite.

At one point, Demara seemed to have found his niche with the Clerics of Saint Viator, a Catholic order of religious brothers and priests in Chicago. Today, the Viatorian Community accepts men and women as lay associates, but when Demara was searching, his focus seemed to be on his calling to become a priest. He'd completed his studies, entering under the weight of French's credentials, though, in all fairness, he pulled off "straight As in rational psychology, metaphysics, cosmology, epistemology, ethics and natural theology." He was ready for ordination, which he told *LIFE* magazine was where he felt truly called. Demara's story ran in the January 28, 1952, issue of *LIFE,* under the title "The Master Impostor, an incredible tale."

"There was nothing I would have liked more," Demara said. "I thought at the time that I had a true religious vocation. But I couldn't go ahead without telling those men the truth about myself. So I disappeared. No explanations. I just disappeared."

It seemed easier for Demara to play at being something or someone, rather than coming clean with his true identity. While he was still using the name French, he accepted a position teaching psychology at Gannon College in Erie, Pennsylvania. From there, he moved to Olympia, Washington, as a psychology professor at St. Martin's College in Lacey. His reputation as a speed-reader with a photographic mind came in handy for these teaching positions, and if one were simply evaluating his prowess as a professor, he would have appeared knowledgeable and capable. "I just kept ahead of the class. The best way to learn anything is to teach it," Demara told *LIFE*.

Demara carved out a nice life for himself in Olympia. He was even made a special constable on campus. But his undercover activities were about to be exposed. It was about this time that the FBI, working for the U.S. Army and Navy, caught up with Demara, and he found himself in a lot of trouble for ditching his military responsibilities. He was charged with "desertion in time of war," a charge that could have resulted in the death penalty. But he used his wit and charm to get away with a six-year prison sentence, which he served at the U.S. Naval Disciplinary Barracks in San Pedro, California. He was out in 18 months because of "mitigating circumstances and good behaviour." During his time in the barracks, Demara worked as an editor for the camp's newspaper. It was a perfect cover for learning everything he could about the way prisons work, and he'd call on this knowledge years later in another incarnation of his personality.

A jail sentence should have dissuaded Demara from assuming future false identities. Not so. After leaving prison, Demara was again poring over old college catalogues. This time, he took on the identity of Dr. Cecil Boyce Hamann, a biologist with Kentucky's Ashbury College. Under that identity, Demara took a job at the Massachusetts Eye and Ear Infirmary, working as an orderly during the day and, in the evenings, studying law, though he had no intention of ever becoming a lawyer. Demara left his legal studies after about a year; he wasn't as interested in becoming a lawyer as he was about learning the law for his own benefit. Once again, he was on the move, this time, using his credentials as Dr. Hamann to gain entry to the Brothers of Christian Instruction in Alfred, Maine. The Brothers gave Demara the religious name of Brother John and sent the new novice to Grand Falls, New Brunswick, to study theology. While in Canada, Demara helped the order establish a college charter so those entering the novitiate didn't have to travel to the University of Montréal for their studies.

Demara first met the good Dr. Cyr while living in Grand Falls, where the physician was treating Demara's teacher, Brother Boniface, for rheumatoid arthritis. As the two became fast friends, Demara learned that the doctor was interested in working in the U.S. Cyr knew Demara as Dr. Hamann or Brother John, and Cyr reasoned that with his medical background, his new American friend might be able to help him get a licence in Maine, so he could practice medicine there as well as in his native country. Demara agreed to do what he could to facilitate the process, and Cyr gave Demara his credentials and personal information. But, instead of following through with Cyr's request, Demara, dejected over the fact that he wasn't chosen to head the school he'd just helped establish, had other plans for Cyr's personal information.

The salty sea air was calling him, once again.

BACK ON THE BRIDGE

The war in Korea had been raging now for nearly a year, and Demara knew that, in any battlefield, doctors were in demand. In March 1951, equipped with Cyr's medical credentials, Demara returned to New Brunswick and presented himself to the Royal Canadian Navy in St. John. "I told them that if they didn't take me in a hurry I'd join the Canadian Army," Demara told *LIFE*. Two hours later, he was on a train to Ottawa, commissioned and enlisted as a surgeon-lieutenant. He worked for the first two months at the naval hospital in Halifax.

It was there that Demara made what he called the biggest mistake of his life—he fell in love.

It was a stupid thing to do, but he just couldn't help himself. The woman, who was never named in any of his interviews and whose name appears to be lost to history, mesmerized him. He knew falling in love couldn't work; you can't lie your way through a marriage. But he let himself dream of a future in which he'd come home from working at his medical practice to home-cooked dinners, one or more little rug rats clamouring for his attention and pleading for their "daddy" to pick them up and a wife greeting him with a warm smile and a hot cup of tea.

And yet, strangely, though Demara was a dreamer who seemed to believe he could do anything, he was reluctant to believe too deeply in this dream. His decision to enter directly into the theatre of war was partly to escape the woman who'd made her way into Demara's every waking thought. Still, Demara couldn't completely shake the hope that the two of them might settle down to a nice, ordinary life. Demara asked her to marry him before leaving for Korea, and, while he was away, his fiancée busily planned their wedding for June 1952.

Demara's optimism surrounding domestic bliss was about to be severely tested but not before he was hailed as a hero.

It was September before Demara was treating more than just minor wounds, colds and the odd case of flu. That fall, the *Cayuga* was one of many war vessels operating in the waters near Chinnampo, North Korea. Sources disagree about some of the details surrounding a junk full of South Korean soldiers that had come alongside the *Cyagua* looking for assistance, but most agree that 19 casualties were on board. The soldiers appeared to have been ambushed and were desperate for medical help. Commander Plomer invited the wounded Koreans onto the *Cayuga*, and Demara took immediate control of the situation. When all the soldiers were on the bridge, Demara and his assistant evaluated each man's condition. They separated the urgent cases from the less-serious ones, and Demara ordered the commander's quarters be made into an operating room.

Demara never wasted a lot of time panicking, despite having every reason to, on this occasion. Sixteen of the soldiers had relatively minor injuries. Cleaning and bandaging wounds, applying small sutures, making the injured comfortable: this was relatively straightforward medicine. But the remaining patients were more challenging. Critical. One patient had been hit in the chest with shrapnel. To save the man's life, Demara would have to remove the piece of metal lodged just a quarter of an inch from his heart. An untrained hand could easily make a wrong move. Demara could end up killing his patient.

Crichton reflected on Demara's state of mind in his book, explaining that Demara was cognizant that he'd never seen the inside of a human body and was smart enough to know that even the slightest slip of the scalpel could cost the man his life. It was likely the first time Demara realized that being an impostor wasn't a harmless game; it could have severe consequences. Yet there he was, the man people were counting on to save the soldier's life. But he couldn't turn back now; strange as it might seem, he was the man's best chance at survival.

Going by the principle that "the less cutting you do, the less patching up you have to do afterwards," as Demara later told *LIFE*, he made the most complicated of operations as simple as possible. He began by cutting into his patient's skin just above the heart and following along the breastbone. Instead of separating the breastbone, Demara moved aside a single fractured rib, spotted the shrapnel, and, with a hand as steady as that of any studied surgeon, removed the metal. After using a coagulating agent to prevent the patient's wound from hemorrhaging and after repairing the internal damage, Demara replaced the rib, stitched the soldier's chest back together and wrapped him in bandages. A couple of hours later, the soldier was sipping soup, anxious to return to duty. Twelve hours after surgery, Demara's once-critical patient walked off the *Cayuga*.

Demara conducted two more similarly difficult surgeries that night. When he finally slipped off his gloves, pulled down his mask and took a stretch, he noticed that all eyes were on him—and had been the entire night. "I couldn't have been nervous, even if I felt like it," Demara told *LIFE*. "Practically everybody on the bloody ship was standing there, watching me." The loveable ship's doctor, who to that point in the journey had little to concern himself with, had become a hero to the men with whom he served.

With their current mission accomplished, the *Cayuga* left the area, but when it returned a week or so later, Demara couldn't resist the temptation to go ashore and check on his patient. The conditions he discovered were devastating, and he was so moved by the lack of medical aid that he gained permission to offer his services for a time. Because the *Cayuga* couldn't be left without some medical representative on board, Demara's assistant remained behind.

Once again, Demara found himself in the middle of various medical emergencies and with even less support than he'd had during his first intense medical experiences on the *Cayuga*. Amputations and combating deadly infections were typical daily concerns, and Demara was gaining confidence with each procedure. One day, his rapidly blossoming skills were tested again, when he came across a young soldier who'd been hit in the chest by a dumdum bullet. These bullets not only pierced through the skin, but they also expanded when they hit their target, causing even more horrific damage to the human body than an ordinary bullet. The wounded man before Demara had what looked like an ordinary bullet hole through the front of his chest and a gaping canyon in his back. Through the wound, Demara could see that the soldier's lung had been made into mincemeat. The only chance for his survival was to remove the lung. In an interesting twist of fate, Demara had just read about a lung resection in the British Medical Journal *The Lancet*. He was ready to proceed.

Again, the patient survived—even thrived after surgery. Weeks after Demara operated, the *Cayuga* returned to the area, and Demara visited his patient. The soldier had lost a lot of blood, both before and after the surgery, but Demara had had no plasma to replace it. Despite the success of the surgery, Demara had little hope of the patient's long-term success. When he found the soldier working in the fields, alongside friends and family, Demara's own heart nearly stopped. "There he was, as big as life, working," Demara told *LIFE*. "It was woman's work, of course, but still he was trying to pull his share of the weight… he saw me, he broke into a big grin…."

Demara was also thriving. With each heady success, his confidence grew, and, in the process, he was developing quite a reputation for himself. In fact, he was becoming something of a Canadian legend, and, before long, reporters were trying to talk him into giving an interview. At first, he managed to elude the press, but part of what kept Demara in the con game was the excitement, and what could be more exciting than to have the media write of your exploits?

One could say that it was Demara's pride, then, that led to his ultimate demise. To be fair, when he finally agreed to an interview with Lieutenant R.A.V. Jenkins, the Canadian Navy's public relations guru responsible for gathering news from the Far East, Demara purposefully downplayed the difficulties of his surgeries and work in Korea. He knew that any kind of press could potentially expose him, but even Demara seemed to underestimate how widely the story of his exploits with the Canadian Navy aboard the *Cayuga* would travel.

And the news did travel, wider and faster than anyone could have imagined.

EXTRA! EXTRA! READ ALL ABOUT IT!

Again, how Demara was finally discovered and reported to the naval authorities as an imposter isn't clear. One suggestion was that Dr. Cyr's mother noticed the articles that were supposed to be about her son and, knowing he wasn't serving in

Korea at the time, reported the deception. Another story claims the real Dr. Cyr, who was working at his practice in Grand Falls, New Brunswick, read the stories that were supposedly written about him and called the authorities.

Neither report jives with the most likely scenario related by other media accounts, which suggest that the real Dr. Cyr was contacted by the RCMP and shown a photograph of Demara. The doctor identified the photo as a snapshot of Dr. Cecil Hamann or Brother John (Cyr still would not have known the man as Demara then). Cyr told the *New Brunswick Telegraph Journal* that, after identifying his one-time friend, he told the RCMP what he thought they should do with Demara. "I told them, for the love of Mike...to leave the man alone. He hasn't hurt anybody."

Along with the rest of the world, over the next few months, Cyr learned of the multiple deceptions Demara had pulled off in his life. And, although Cyr wouldn't have chosen to have his identity stolen, he defended Demara's motives. Cyr thought perhaps the man suffered from a mental illness, was quite possibly a megalomaniac, for example. "There was something wrong with the way he thought about things, no doubt about it," Cyr told Glenn Allen of the *Telegraph Journal*, "[but] there was something charming about the man. He was quite a character. And I don't think he ever hurt anybody and may have even done some good in his life."

Regardless of his success, and the soft spot the general public seemed to have for him, Demara's actions still embarrassed the Royal Canadian Navy. When Demara spoke with *LIFE* in January 1952, just months after his return to the U.S., he said he could still hear Commander Plomer read the urgent radio message he'd received from Ottawa. It read: "We have information that Joseph C. Cyr, surgeon-lieutenant, 0-17669, is an imposter. Remove from active duty immediately, repeat immediately, conduct investigation and report facts to Chief of Naval Staff Ottawa." Some stories suggested that Demara fell apart when he heard the news; other stories claimed that, like every other time he'd been uncovered, he took it all in stride. Regardless, reports uniformly agree that Demara's shipmates' opinion of the man they'd met just months before, and had so quickly learned to love, didn't falter.

Nevertheless, Demara couldn't go on serving as a doctor. He was officially discharged from service on November 21, 1951. In his book, *Thunder in the Morning Calm*, author Edward C. Meyers describes how officials handled the Demara case. He explained that the Canadian government thought it best to forget the entire incident and discharge Demara as quickly as possible. Demara was paid the money he was owed—despite not having the credentials to serve as a doctor, he was remarkably competent, and, in the eyes of his superiors, he had earned his wage—and was transported to the U.S. Immigration Office in Blaine, Washington. Because there were no outstanding warrants on Demara in the U.S., he was released from custody.

And so it was that the charming, disarming navy doctor that Canada was so proud of went home to the U.S.

It was not the last that the world would see of Ferdinand Waldo Demara.

After Korea

Once Demara got over the disappointment of leaving the post he so thoroughly enjoyed, having felt the most useful serving in the Canadian Navy than he ever had in his entire life, he was faced with yet another sad reality. There was someone waiting for him; a young woman was planning her future, and it included a walk down the aisle with the man she knew and loved as Dr. Cyr. "I knew that I would never be able to face her after all this and I imagined what she was thinking about me. It just about killed me," Demara told *LIFE*. Although he pined for the woman he loved, he didn't elaborate on how the situation ended.

Smarting from the loss of the love of his life, the loss of a job that in many ways defined him, the loss of his colleagues' respect and the loss of any personal direction, no matter how tenuous his life had been, Demara slid into a period of heavy drinking. Previously a teetotaller, Demara returned to the home of his youth, in Lawrence, Massachusetts, and mourned. "I couldn't get that girl out of my head. And I kept thinking about how happy I was in the Canadian Navy. I guess I was happier there than I had been anywhere in my life."

He hadn't decided what he was going to do next. He admitted that assuming his various roles would be "a tough habit to break"—how could he be content merely living life as Ferdinand Demara? He also admitted that he still wasn't ready to make his way through life the way everyone else in the world was expected to—by studying, working and climbing the ladder of success on one's own steam.

But he had a few ideas.

For a time, he used his previous, and only, prison experience and the accounting and business administration skills of a man named Ben W. Jones to land a position at Huntsville prison. He started out as a guard, but his innovative ideas, which revolved around rehabilitating the men by providing them with education and physical recreation, were noticed. It wasn't long before Demara was promoted to deputy warden.

Finally, he was bouncing back and taking charge. Although he was still using someone else's identity, he was also making a difference in the world. But happenstance would play havoc with Demara's plans. He noticed an inmate reading the issue of *LIFE* magazine that contained his story. Again, stories differ over what happened next. Some suggested Demara played his old disappearing act and left before he was confronted. Other stories say he was confronted and simply released from his duties with no further action taken, to reduce the potential for embarrassment for the Texas prison system. Either way, it was the end of another career.

From there, Demara returned to Maine or, more specifically, to an island off the coast of Maine, where he worked as a teacher under the name of Marin Godgart. The kids loved him. He loved the kids. Again, success and happiness seemed well within his grasp, and again he was discovered. Although *LIFE* had paid him $2500 for the exclusive, it was becoming increasingly obvious that almost everyone read the magazine, and those who didn't read other publications describing Demara's story. As long as his story was in the public eye, Demara would continue to be routed out of whatever role he was playing.

So it was goodbye to Maine and hello to a cross-continent run that took him to northern Alaska. Still masquerading as Marin Godgart, Demara got himself another job. But, as luck would have it, people in the wilds of Alaska read *LIFE* too, and a trapper Demara met discovered him.

There were other jobs under other names. Newspaper banners were again screaming headlines about unmasking the "Genius without Portfolio." Demara ran from Alaska to Mexico to Cuba and all points U.S.A., and, for the next several years, it seemed he couldn't stay anywhere for long. Someone would always identify him.

And then Demara disappeared.

THE LAST STOP ON THE TOUR

In 1959, Demara telephoned Crichton. He'd worked closely with the author in the writing of *The Great Impostor* and had provided feedback on the movie that was made from the book. Demara probably thought Crichton was one of the only friends he had in the world. He was "on the biggest caper of them all," Demara told Crichton. Demara didn't elaborate.

It was the last Crichton heard from him.

For two decades, Demara dropped out of the headlines. No one seemed to know where he was, what he was doing or if he was even alive.

But then, in 1980, as Dr. Cyr was making his rounds in a hospital in Anaheim, California, he noticed a face that triggered memories from the past. "It couldn't be," Cyr said to himself. It took a little time, but eventually Cyr met up with Demara for the third time in his life. "He was working as the non-denominational hospital chaplain," Cyr told the *New Brunswick Telegraph Journal*. "We didn't discuss the old days. Every morning he'd greet me with the words 'Good morning Dr. Cyr.' But there was no doubt that he recognized me. He knew that I knew… I didn't think he was harming anybody—I saw no need [to turn him in]."

Demara lived out his last days working as a chaplain at that hospital. Although he certainly felt some sense of pleasure comforting the sick, his rather staid life couldn't compare to the exhilarating years of his youth, and, at times, that surely depressed him. Demara's own physician told the *New York Times* that his patient was "the most miserable, unhappy man I have ever known." Demara died of a heart attack in 1982. He was just 61, and he left no family to mourn his loss.

There's no definitive list of Demara's aliases nor of the jobs he acquired over time. But in 1999, the *Ottawa Citizen* took an impressive stab at doing just that. According to the *Citizen,* in addition to the names and titles already mentioned in this story, Demara was a "director of publications at St. Martin's Washington; a science instructor at a boys' school in Arkansas; a graduate of William and Mary, Virginia; an English teacher; a Catholic Brother at Trappist and other monasteries in 10 states and in Canada; a college founder at Notre Dame Normal School; a Maine junior college instructor; a cancer researcher with the Christian Brothers Order; a hotel auditor in Houston; a Latin Master at North Haven High School in Maine, and an English teacher among Inuit at Point Barrow, Alaska."

Like any other con artist, Demara was successful because he knew how to gain the confidence of the men and women he met. He knew that the recipe for success included liberal doses of flattery, and he was a professional liar. But unlike most con artists, he genuinely loved the people who came into his life—all of them. He only ever accepted money that he had earned, and, according to the majority of his supervisors, he was viewed as a valuable employee.

At one point, Demara told *LIFE* that, "In this little game I was playing there always comes a time when you find yourself getting in too deep. You've made good friends who believe in you, and you don't want them to get hurt and disillusioned. You begin to worry about what they'll think if somebody exposes you as a phony."

Even though he loved the thrill, it wasn't enough, but life without the thrill of the run and chase didn't satisfy him, either. In either case, Demara's story is certainly unique. There's really not another tale like it...much like the man himself.

Notes on Sources

Information for stories throughout this text was retrieved from many sources, including several community news outlets, online and print publications and special interest groups: *Calgary Herald, Calgary Sun, Canadian Christianity, Canadian Mennonite,* CBC, Court TV, CNN, *Dateline, Edmonton Sun, Edmonton Journal, Elle Canada, Globe and Mail,* KOMO 4 News, Library and Archives Canada, *LIFE* magazine, *Mennonite Weekly Review, New York Post, Vancouver Province, Reader's Digest,* CBC News, *New York Times, People* magazine, *Psychology Today, Smithers Interior News,* Statistics Canada, the Guardian Unlimited, *The East Hampton Star, Pensacola News Journal, Vancouver Sun, Vancouver Province, Vanity Fair, W-FIVE,* Wikipedia.com, *Winnipeg Free Press, Winnipeg Sun, 60 Minutes,* B.C. Securities Commission, Competition Bureau Canada, Lakewood Public Library Women in History, U.S. Securities and Exchange Commission.

Bankers Online
www.bankersonline.com/articles/bhv01n03/bhv01n03a13.html

The Law Office of Crotty and Saland
www.new-york-lawyers.org/lawyer-attorney-1311915.html

Aga Khan Foundation
www.akfc.ca/

CFB Esquimalt Naval & Military Museum
www.navalandmilitarymuseum.org/resource_pages/chars/
demara.html

The RCMP's *Personal Information and Scams Protection—A Canadian Practical Guide*
www.rcmp-grc.gc.ca/scams-fraudes/canad-practical-pratique-guide-eng.htm

Alexander Keith
Larabee, Ann. *The Dynamite Fiend.* Halifax: Nimbus Publishing Ltd., 2005.

Ferdinand Waldo Demara
McCarthy, Joe. "The Master Impostor: An Incredible Tale." *LIFE* magazine, January 28, 1952.

The Great Impostor, a movie based on the novel by Robert Crichton, directed by Robert Mulligan, 1961.

Christophe Rocancourt
Dateline NBC

www.msnbc.msn.com/id/11770944/ns/dateline_nbc/

Lisa Wojna

Bestselling author Lisa Wojna has at least 24 non-fiction books to her credit, including two others with Quagmire Press: *Missing! The Disappeared, Lost or Abducted in Canada* and *Unsolved Murders of Canada*. She has worked in the community newspaper industry as a writer and journalist and has travelled all over Canada, from the windy prairies of Manitoba to northern British Columbia, and even to the wilds of Africa. Although writing and photography have been a central part of her life for as long as she can remember, it's the people behind every story that are her motivation and give her the most fulfilment.

Check out more True Crime from

QUAGMIRE PRESS

GANGS IN CANADA
by Jeff Pearce

In *Gangs in Canada*, Jeff Pearce draws a portrait of a crime wave spreading across the country and infecting our youth. He shows how police, ex-gang members and organizations are reclaiming our young people and showing them ways out of a violent, doomed lifestyle. This is the most gripping, up-to-date chronicle of what is happening on our streets.

HC $29.95/PB $18.95 • ISBN: HC 978-1-926695-10-5
PB 978-1-926695-07-5 • 5.25" x 8.25" • 208 pages

DEADLY CANADIAN WOMEN
The Stories Behind the Crimes of Canada's Most Notorious Women
by Patricia MacQuarrie

Some Canadian women have done the unthinkable and murdered spouses, lovers, children, even complete strangers. These women are from across Canada and across social backgrounds, and many of their cases have changed the Canadian criminal justice system. This book tells their stories.

$18.95 • ISBN: 978-0-9783409-2-6 • 5.25" x 8.25" • 256 pages

WRONGFULLY CONVICTED
The Innocent in Canada
by Peter Boer

From David Milgaard to Wilbert Coffin, the six men whose stories are told in this book suffered at the hands of the Canadian justice system.

$18.95 • ISBN: 978-0-9783409-1-9 • 5.25" x 8.25" • 256 pages

**Available from your local bookseller or by contacting the distributor,
Lone Pine Publishing
1-800-661-9017
www.lonepinepublishing.com**